Endorsements

"*Experiencing God's Love in the Church* presents an insightful, and often painful, analysis of the modern church fellowship, one that has too often 'lost the battle for relevance and is no longer distinguishable from other nonprofit community organizations.' Not content merely to identify a problem, Blackaby reveals the root cause as a lack of genuine love in the church and offers real examples of how lovelessness manifests itself in a church body. With the keen insight of an experienced pastor he offers specific guidance on reclaiming lost love. Only when this true love is manifest will the world be drawn to the God of love. This book should be read and applied by pastors and churches everywhere."
—**Richard L. Blake,** *founder/president, Xtend Ministries International*

"'When love is evident in a church, God lives there among His people.' With this statement Tom Blackaby shows how to experience God through loving others. His prophetic assessment of the state of many churches today brought tears to my eyes as the truth convicted me, as it will our culture. Then, as a modern prophet, he calls me back to a loving God with practical suggestions for redemption. The book is a must for church leaders and all who desire to experience God in a more dynamic way."
—**Cal Dunlap,** *executive director, Association for Christian Conferences, Teaching, and Service*

"There are few topics more pressing for the North American church today than how to experience and express the love of Christ. I believe this book provides practical insights coupled with relevant examples and application suggestions that can assist any church in evaluating its effectiveness in fulfilling Christ's command to love each other. If God's people are going to impact their communities, cities, and nations as God intended us to do, I believe we must get a handle on what it means to showcase the inexplicable love of Christ in our midst. I am grateful that this book helps us do that."

—**Dr. Robert D. Blackaby,** *president, Canadian Southern Baptist Seminary and College*

"Many Christians in America today question the vitality of the church. Tom Blackaby identifies what's missing, but more importantly tells us how to fix it! This book is written to encourage Christians to love each other, and in so doing, impact the world around them. It is a simple message of the church letting its light shine and being used by God to accomplish His purposes. It's right on target for where we are today and is a must-read for Christians who want to see revival in our land."

—**Robert L. Mitchell,** *chairman, Fellowship of Companies for Christ International*

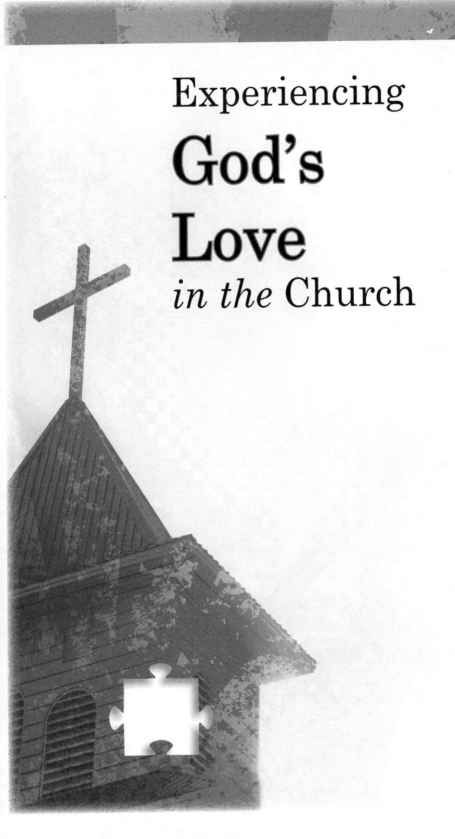

Experiencing
God's
Love
in the Church

Experiencing
God's
Love
in the Church

**The Missing
Ingredient in
Today's Church
and How to
Bring It Back**

TOM BLACKABY

NEW HOPE
PUBLISHERS
Birmingham, Alabama

New Hope® Publishers
P. O. Box 12065
Birmingham, AL 35202-2065
www.newhopepublishers.com
New Hope Publishers is a division of WMU®.

Library of Congress Cataloging-in-Publication Data

Blackaby, Tom, 1962-
  Experiencing God's love in the church : the missing ingredient in today's church and how to bring it back / Tom Blackaby.
    p. cm.
  ISBN 978-1-59669-296-1 (sc)
  1. Love--Religious aspects--Christianity. 2. Church. I. Title.
  BV4639.B52 2011
  241'.4--dc22

                         2010033535

ISBN-10: 1-59669-296-0
ISBN-13: 978-1-59669-296-1

N114133 • 1210 • 4M1

Dedication

This book is written with love and admiration for the many fine Christians who have shown my family and me God's love over the years, and to two churches in particular who know what it means to love one another deeply: North Sea Baptist Church and Cornerstone Neighbourhood Church.

Table of Contents

Preface

At this point in my life I have now served God's people in ministry for more than 25 years. I have been a youth pastor, minister of music, religious education pastor, associate pastor, senior pastor, and a national consultant to churches for worship and religious education. I have lived in three countries and traveled in about 27 others, often speaking to churches, seminaries, and Christian organizations. I say, as my father once said to me, God's people are the best people in the world!

Over the years my best friends have always come from churches that I have attended, as have innumerable fond and blessed memories. As I write this, the oldest of my three children has just begun her first year of college. I can honestly say that I never once have had to cajole, threaten, or bribe my three children to go to church—because they love going. And that is how it should be. The joy on the faces of believers I have worshipped with in remote African villages, crowded cities in India, international churches in the Middle East, and right across Europe and the Americas affirms to me that Jesus is alive and well in the hearts of His people. It has been a great privilege to walk with godly and inspiring Christians around the world.

On the other hand, I have also had many painful and challenging times working with God's people in churches. Some of God's people have tremendously blessed me and my family, greatly encouraging me at very important times. Others have caused me to question why I ever entered the ministry in the first place! As one brother in Christ once said to me, "Sheep can bite." I have learned that to be true. Yet still God chooses to use His people to bring hope and truth and grace and peace in desperate times. And although there are some people who profess to be "Christian" without any clue to what that really means, far more are quietly showing God's love wherever they go and lives are being transformed around them because of it.

Really, though, it is not my opinion that matters; it is only Christ's opinion that truly counts. We are His people, the sheep of His pasture. We are His body, His church, and His chosen method for sharing the good news of salvation with those who are perishing. May we represent Him well in all that we do and say, and embody the fact that God loves the world and that God sent His Son as a demonstration of that love.

—TWB

Experiencing God's Love in the Church

■ ■ ■

Ah, to wake up Sunday morning anticipating
a glorious meeting with God joined by your brothers
and sisters in Christ!

■ ■ ■

Chapter 1

Love Desired

Ah, to wake up Sunday morning anticipating a glorious meeting with God joined by your brothers and sisters in Christ!

Your spouse and children get in the car early because they don't want to miss anything, and you know if you don't arrive a bit early you won't get seats together in the auditorium. You park a block away from church because so many people are coming to see what God is up to this week. It is a challenge getting to the auditorium because so many people want to shake your hand and ask how your week has been. A woman from the prayer team hands you a card with a Bible verse printed on it and a handwritten note below: "We've been praying for you and your father in the hospital." You wonder how she found out! Open seats are few and far between, but you find a new family to sit with and you introduce yourself to them. They are new to the community and heard about your church from friends, so you offer to buy them lunch after the service. Throughout the service people sense the Spirit working in their hearts, leading them and guiding them in areas of their lives where they need direction. You're certain the pastor's message is from the Lord as your questions about taking that job in a different town are answered. You decide you'd rather take a pay cut than leave this church where God is so obviously at work, the staff are so godly and inspiring, and the people are so loving and caring towards one another. By the time the pastor finishes, the front of the auditorium is packed with people who have come to quietly kneel before God in prayer. The music softly plays as people continue to pray. Some are quietly weeping, others just kneeling, and a few have friends who came to support them with a hand on their shoulder. You have no doubt that the coming week is going to be great, and you even begin to wonder what God has in store for you the next Sunday!

For many Christians, this is their normal experience at church. But for other believers who coast from Sunday to Sunday and from church to church, this experience is quite foreign to them.

Perhaps a different scenario is more familiar to you. A situation more like Kelly's. Kelly wakes up on Sunday morning, looks at the alarm clock and gauges how much time she will need to get her family up and dressed, fed, and in the car to get to church on time. With only minor resistance, her family piles into the car—all with matching socks and combed hair! As she drives into the church parking lot searching for a space not too far from the building, she waves, nods, and smiles at the people she recognizes. Two of her children forgot their Bibles, but as they are only occasionally used anyway, that won't be a big problem. The kids run off to be with their friends, compare action figures, and chat about the weekend activities. She and her husband do the familiar "meet and greet" routine as they walk through the foyer towards the auditorium.

Kelly wonders if today will be any different than the past weeks or months. Perhaps the choir or praise team will do something unexpected today. Maybe there will be a video presentation she hasn't seen before. As Kelly enters the worship center she scans for seats that will accommodate her family—not a problem, as there are many open spots. She wishes there were some sense of anticipation or building expectation in her heart for worship today, but no luck. She glances at the people around her and notices a few faces she doesn't recognize. She wonders if they are new or if she just hasn't noticed them before. No matter, her life is too busy to add any new friends to it, and they may not come back to the church again anyway, so there's no point getting to know them yet.

During the morning announcements she hears something about a church picnic next Saturday, but as she doesn't really have any close friends in the church it's always a bit awkward going to such events. She remembers last year when the only people who spoke to her were the church's paid staff. She reasons that this is probably typical of most churches—that's just the way church is in these busy times. Of course there are the usual mentions of fund-raising events for building projects and a prayer request for the ethnic mission church that meets in the afternoons. She appreciates the effort that the pastor puts in his sermons, but somehow they just don't seem to hit home, and her mind wanders to the coming week's events, schedules, and responsibilities. The service runs like clockwork through the singing, the offering, the announcements, the message, and the closing songs. Her family gets out right on time, as usual.

Back in the car Kelly realizes that she did not have any personal conversations with anyone beyond the usual "How are you?" No one asked how well her dad is recovering in the hospital. No one knows about the financial strain her family is facing and her growing anxiety about the future of her business. No one knows how much she would love to have someone pray with her about the possibility of relocating her family to a friendlier economic environment, but she doesn't know who to ask or who to trust. She is not even really sure she wants to expose her personal life to others who may only gossip about her later. But, of course, Kelly acknowledges she is just as unaware of what is going on in the lives of all the other smartly dressed people she saw at the church.

Variations of Kelly's routine happen every week in many churches across the country and around the world. In our hearts we know that church is important and that God should be a priority in our family's life, but there is this nagging feeling that there should be something more to it than the regular Sunday routine, more than simply smiling back at smiling people you see once a week, more than singing songs, standing, sitting, bowing heads, taking Communion, and giving an offering. Many people sit in their seats asking, "Why did I come to church today?" but the answer remains elusive.

Over the years, I have served churches in many different locations, and in many different job descriptions. I have been on staff as the youth pastor, the minister of religious education, the worship pastor, and the senior pastor. And in every church in which I have served, I have looked for the one ingredient that seems to bring it all together—love.

Let Us Love One Another

Dear friends, let us continually love one another, because love comes from God. Everyone who loves has been born from God and knows God. The person who does not love does not know God, because God is love.
—1 John 4:7–8 (ISV)

Perhaps you have this verse engraved on a plaque on your wall or written on some furniture in your church. Some of us have studied this passage, reflected over its meaning, and even taught it to our children. But there is a vast difference between knowing the Bible and living it out in our daily life. Understanding the far-reaching implications of this verse is part of what this book is about, but that is only half of it. The goal of this book is not simply to provide more knowledge, but to help us live out what Christ expects of us in our daily lives. 1 John 4:7–8 clearly states that whether or not a person loves is the evidence for whether he or she actually knows God. And, if a person is not known for

Experiencing God's Love in the Church

his or her love, then it is impossible for them to truly know God, regardless of what they say.

I am often astonished at the fanciful mental gymnastics some people employ to explain why they feel it is impossible to implement Scripture in their daily lives. They seek to relegate Scripture to some ultimate ideal or unachievable virtue that Christ alone can conquer. I am of the persuasion that if God gives a command, we either obey or we don't. He isn't interested in 43 reasons why we think His commands are unreasonable, impractical, or impossible; He is interested only in our obedience. When God says, "Let us love one another," He actually means it in real and practical terms.

This book is written to encourage God's people to love one another as Christ expects them to.

There is no question that the church (universal and local) is struggling in a fallen world today. In many cases the church has lost the battle for relevance and is no longer distinguishable from other nonprofit community organizations. The farther we get chronologically from the original New Testament churches, the less we seem to look like them. A disconnect has occurred between what we read of Christ's expectations for His body (the church) and what actually happens in the buildings where His people meet week after week.

This book seeks to go back to the beginning, to look once again at the biblical narrative, at the commands of Christ, at the instructions of the apostles—to use them as a plumb line against which we can place our own church. What adjustments need to be made in our thinking and actions in order to comply with our Lord's expectations for us? This book is in no way an exhaustive look at love. Rather it is a primer to help us examine where we are and discover where we need to be.

There are many significant books written on the importance of loving God, and rightfully so. There are also many must-read books exhorting God's people to creatively love and reach out to those who are not yet Christians. This book is written to encourage God's people to love one another as Christ expects them to, so that He can accomplish His will and purposes through them and touch a watching world around them.

Do We Really Understand What Love Is?

For the whole law is summarized in a single statement:
"You must love your neighbor as yourself."
—Galatians 5:14 (ISV)

This is an incredible verse. I have preached it, taught it, discussed it, and pondered it over the years, as many of you have. And it grieves me to see how little it is practiced in churches today. We work together on projects, we run summer children's programs together, provide community outreach events, even study the Bible and worship side by side, but when we look at the person across the aisle from us at church, can we honestly say that we truly love that person or that family? I hope so.

- I wonder if everyone in our churches would feel perfectly comfortable calling up any other church member at a moment's notice to ask for help or urgent prayer for a situation they are facing.

- I wonder if each person in the church feels that they are an important and integral part of their church family and knows they are loved unconditionally by the other members.

- I wonder if people know they will be fervently prayed for and not gossiped about, carefully listened to rather than criticized behind their backs, purposefully sought out rather than run off, or diligently pursued rather than quietly let go.

There are many wonderful churches that demonstrate what it means both to love the Lord God with all their heart, soul, strength, and mind and to love one another genuinely as Christ has loved them. They understand how to care for and nurture the sheep in their community of faith. But other churches really struggle with both of the great commandments (Matthew 22:37–39). The fact is, if you have trouble loving one another, then you also have trouble loving God (1 John 4:20–21).

I have traveled in 13 countries in the past two years and I have yet to see the two great commandments posted in any church to remind God's people of their foremost priorities. Maybe it is just easier not to be reminded of our high calling. The church is the one place where, more than any other, a man or woman, boy or girl, should be able to walk through the doors and find love—guaranteed. The one immediate and obvious difference between a church and every other organization, club, society, or company ought to be sacrificial, undying, genuine love. Why? Since God lives in and among His people, we ought to reflect His love for those for whom He sent His Son to die. It is tragic when this is not the case.

The Good, the Bad, and the Model

As I grew up, my family rarely lived near any close relatives, so the churches we attended supplied our friends, our playmates, our co-workers, our brothers and sisters in Christ, our "grandparents," and, for two of us, our wives! As children and teenagers, we loved our church family, and they loved us. My earliest memories of what church is all about centered on the two greatest commandments of loving God and loving one another. So, ever since, I have been on a journey seeking to find or establish the same kind of loving relationships in every church in which I have served or attended.

Over the years I have seen love demonstrated in some amazing ways, both love for God and love for people. I watched a church wrap its arms around a man whose wife was dying from cancer and hold prayer vigils for his family right through to the end. I know a church that bought and installed a wood-burning stove in a widow's home to keep her from freezing in the winter and had wood regularly delivered to her house at no cost to her. I was a part of a church that provided a wedding and reception for a poor couple with no family. People even volunteered to serve as the "father" of the bride and the groom's best man!

But sadly, I could tell you horror stories that defy logic, grace, common sense, and any semblance of love. I witnessed a chairman of deacons taunt a Sunday School director and demand they "go outside to settle this once and for all." I know about sexual abuse by youth pastors, marital affairs among church leadership, unjustified staff firings, pastors abusing their authority, embezzlement by church treasurers, intimidation from church leaders, swindlers cheating church members, unrestrained pride, unmitigated arrogance, power-tripping, political maneuvering, manipulation, and much more.

While there are many wonderful things that I'm sure Christ would be proud to see in His churches, there are also many things going on that sadden and even disgust Him. What has happened to His churches? Why are so many churches so far away from what He desires them to be? Where did it all go so wrong?

Many years ago, I was introduced to a church in which members fervently and systematically studied the Word of God together, cherished their times of fellowship with one another, regularly shared meals with one another, and promoted and protected their time of corporate prayer. Not surprisingly, in this same church the presence and power of the Holy Spirit was so evident that miraculous things were regularly reported in answer to their constant prayers. I also heard that in this congregation no member ever went without because those who had more than enough quickly shared what they had with those who were in need. The welfare and wellbeing of each member had the highest priority among the membership. They also had an incredible sense of unity and often visited in one another's homes to encourage one another.

What is more, this church was known for its meaningful, personal, and exhilarating worship and for exuberant singing of heartfelt praises to God whenever they got together, whether it was in their homes or in their church. I heard they always displayed such joy and were so grateful to God that visitors could not help but be inspired when they were around them. It is not that they had a life of ease, for in fact their members were often confronted by hostile business leaders and even suffered outright persecution in their communities. Yet they remained steadfast in their love for God and for one another.

It is not surprising to know that this church grew by leaps and bounds as God richly blessed them and helped them reach their community with the gospel. Apparently they faced some potentially divisive issues, but they valued their unity so much that they quickly met to resolve the problems so they would not be distracted or diverted from accomplishing God's purposes. I hope this sounds a *lot* like your church! It sure sounds to me like a great church for my family to attend!

It had all the things we are looking for in a church: Bible-based teaching, a strong fellowship, practical ministry, and deep love for one another. A place where people are the priority, where there is intimacy with God and openness with one another, and where they are making a real difference in their community and around the world. I wonder how they were able to achieve all this with the pressures of society, the demands on people's time, and the many things that competed for their attention. This church sounds like the ideal place for families to go and for Christians young and old to be nurtured and discipled.

The church I'm describing is (as you likely guessed) the first church in Jerusalem, which formed following Christ's ascension and is described in Acts 2. And in the more than 30 countries I've visited, I've found, sadly, that this kind of church is pretty rare.

My Current Journey

Let me give you some background. After serving 15 years on staff in three churches, I served for seven years as pastor of an international congregation in Norway that looked a lot like the Jerusalem church to me. It was filled with people from all over the world who came together to worship the Lord and serve God together. Though we all spoke English as a common language, our cultures, denominational backgrounds, nationalities, and church histories were all different. What was fascinating to me was how we were able to put aside petty differences and personal agendas or preferences in order to worship and serve our Lord together and become family to one another.

But coming "home" from overseas after nearly a decade of being away was definitely a shock to our spiritual lives. For the first time in our married life, my wife and I had to search for a church home. Previously I had always served on staff in each of the churches we attended. We began searching for a place where we could become a part of a spiritual family, a church where the members would care for us and give us opportunities to use our gifts in service and ministry. However, the search for a church home in our new community was frustrating, disappointing, and at times agonizing. I still remember the quizzical look on our children's faces each Sunday morning (and occasionally Saturday evening) when they would ask, "So which church are we going to today?"

In several churches we attended no one but the official "greeters" welcomed us or introduced themselves to us in the service. We deliberately lingered in the lobby for a while after each service and waited in vain for someone who would talk to us or make us feel welcome or wanted. We decided to visit one church over a longer period of time, but week after week we went home wishing someone would invite our family over to their home or even to join them for lunch after church. No one ever did. So we began attending a home group and getting involved in the praise team ministry. Still no one invited our family into their home, out for coffee, or even to join them at a restaurant after church. We then volunteered to lead study groups in our home, and my wife became integrally involved in various church ministries. But even after 18 months, we did not feel welcomed into the church family. We realized this church had looked great on the outside but lacked love on the inside. So we continued in our search for a church that knew how to "love one another."

In our pursuit of a loving congregation, our search included both small mission churches and larger, more established churches in several different denominations. There didn't seem to be a lot of difference between them, despite their various names, denominational affiliations, catchy mission statements, and designs to reach out in the community. I often wondered to myself why some of these smaller struggling churches even existed, until I learned many of them were comprised almost completely of people who were dissatisfied or disgruntled with the larger established churches!

When I looked over their Sunday bulletins, I wondered what God must think about all their busy programs and ministries designed to attract newcomers while existing members were slipping out the back door family by family. One church saw more than 200 of its members leave because of the drastic changes their new pastor unapologetically made. Two hundred people! This pastor had lost his shepherd's heart, and people were seen as a means to build his kingdom. "Get on board or get off the train" was his mantra. No joke! Where had "Love your neighbor as yourself" gone? Where was Christ's command that those who want to be first must become the servant of all (Mark 9:35)? What about Christ's command to Peter, *"Do you love Me?...Feed My lambs...Feed My sheep"* (John 21:15–17)? In the busyness of "doing for" God, somewhere along the way they had lost their love for one another.

It took us nearly two years to find a church where we felt like we were accepted and loved. It was a quaint little congregation meeting in a community hall down the street from our house. Though we had driven by their little sandwich sign on the sidewalk several times, we had never thought to stop in. When we finally visited their worship service, we were drawn in by their warmth and genuine Christianity. My son was asked to play drums for the worship band (even though they had six drummers already!), and my wife was asked to lead a women's Bible study and help lead their very first women's retreat. Others picked my children up for weekly youth and children's activities, and I was hired by the church to assist with administration and plan their grand opening as a new church in the community. When I think of how this church has accepted our family into their congregation and been such a tremendous blessing to us, tears well up in my eyes even as I write this. It was like going from being orphans with no one to love us to being adopted by a loving, caring family. It would truly break my heart to ever have to leave this church family.

What's Our Witness?

I want to hold a mirror up to see how visitors, whether Christians or not, (and sometimes even those within the church) see us. When God draws someone to a church for the first time, it can be a very daunting experience for them. Sometimes we, God's people, are so focused on our own church culture, traditions, and inside jokes that we unknowingly put up invisible walls that outsiders must somehow leap over in order to become a part of our "spiritual club." We have pampered our sacred cows for so long that we have forgotten there is a whole array of other creatures out there to care for.

My mother spoke of a church she attended where my father was the guest speaker. Often my father is required to sit with the staff before the service begins, leaving my mother to find a seat on her own. She made herself comfortable near the front where Dad could not possibly miss her if he looked for her while preaching. Suddenly a woman came up to her quite agitated and chided my mother for sitting in her favorite place. Now my mother is not a woman to be trifled with. So rather than moving, my mother replied, "Well, thank you for letting me sit in your place today." The woman was obviously not happy, but reluctantly found another place to sit, complaining as she did. After my mother was later introduced as the wife of their internationally renowned guest speaker, this woman hurried over and said to her, "Oh, it's OK that you are sitting in my place today."

Church was never, ever meant to be a private club.

What if it were a distraught mother whose daughter was missing, instead of my mother, who was confronted by this woman? What if it were a young couple who had just miscarried their first child? What if it were a teenager who had been abused the night before and was there searching for God? Would they have left feeling that church was a place where arrogant, proud, and irritating people dress up to gather each week and sing ancient songs?

We expect newcomers to decipher archaic religious language, find secret passages in an unfamiliar Bible, sing strangely written songs from a hymnal without any instructions of what "stanzas" are, and put money in an offering plate that goes who knows where. Then we offer those oh-so-helpful hints that they might want to wear a tie or a dress the next time they come to church. Or perhaps we suggest they put their children in the care of complete strangers so they don't disturb the sleeping people around them next time. Church was never, ever meant to be a private club, or a secret fraternity of religious converts. It was meant to be a family for those needing care, comfort, guidance, encouragement, support, and love.

One of the major premises of my father's book *Experiencing God: Knowing and Doing the Will of God* is that "God is always at work around you." This means that God Himself causes people to come to your church. It means He is working in their hearts to want to serve Him using their spiritual gifts. It means He is constantly preparing His people for opportunities of ministry and service all around them and around the world. He never stops drawing people to Himself, and what better place to bring them than to Christ's body, the church? For here they will find love, hope, purpose, and a spiritual family of brothers and sisters.

Sadly, many Christians are completely oblivious to what their heavenly Father is doing all around them. They are so caught up in their own plans and activities that they have developed spiritual blinders on their eyes. Their hearts are barricaded to what the Spirit may want to do through them. Their minds are closed to any new or creative opportunities to reach the community or minister to Christ's body, the church.

What am I talking about?

- Have you ever seen the director of an Easter musical intimidate and alienate everyone he was working with in order to make the program perfect for the visitors? I have.

- Have you ever worked with a praise team leader who was so arrogant and demanding that she made her musicians cry during rehearsals? I have.

- Have you ever seen the decorations director return to the church after the volunteers had left and "fix" all the things that were not done as well as she could have done them? I have.

- Have you ever seen the food coordinator set someone's pumpkin pie aside at the Thanksgiving dinner because it did not look as pretty as the other pies on the dessert table? I have.

- Do you know a family that was left off the email invitation for the home group party because they didn't quite "fit in" with the other couples? I do.

It is too easy to be so caught up in programs, ministries, projects, and productions that we forget about the very people God called us to serve. No wonder there are so many disgruntled and dissatisfied Christians wandering from church to church to church looking for a spiritual family who will simply love them. Some churches seem to have every conceivable program and ministry—they look so exciting and purposeful on the outside—but lack the one main ingredient that should permeate everything they do: love.

Let me share what happened to an acquaintance of mine, which poignantly sums up what I'm saying. During the worship service my friend felt overwhelmed because of the life issues he was facing and he began to sob where he sat. He needed someone to care, to encourage Him that God would help him through his situation. Many people, including one of the pastors, noticed him weeping. Yet not one person came beside him to pray with him or gently put an arm on his shoulder. He left that day feeling embarrassed and humiliated and since that day has not gone back to his church. Had one person put an arm around him, cried with him, prayed with him, spoke words of support to him, or simply quietly stood next to him, he would have been encouraged and strengthened in his faith and felt loved by his church. But no one did.

Building Barriers to Love

Before I go on, I'd like to address some excuses I've heard to justify what I consider unloving behavior in the church.

- *"We demand excellence in all we do,"* church leaders cry as if it were a Scripture verse. The problem is that "excellence" is often defined by the standards of those demanding it, not by God. God requires holiness and perfection, but not excellence in this sense. "Excellence" leaves the 99 percent of the people who cannot match up in the dust, while those setting the standard for what excellence is are the only ones who can attain it. Wouldn't you rather be known for your overwhelming and unflinching love for one another than for excellence? The truth is, this kind of excellence does not impress God, but seeks to impress the people who come to church, most of whom can never meet the criterion themselves.

■ *"Out with the old and in with the new"* is the war cry of many worship leaders today. I watch as older members struggle to keep up with the words and learn the new rhythms, wondering if they will ever hear a familiar song again. Don't get me wrong; I am the first one to jump in and play the drum set if the drummer doesn't show up, but there has to be a way to honor every person in the family, not simply discard those who can't keep up. Gearing worship services to attract outsiders while the insiders feel abandoned is unloving. Love won't allow people to be left behind.

■ *"Youth need separate buildings, separate discipling, separate worship,"* say the youth pastors, while homes are disintegrating and families are breaking up all over the church. Some families are out every night of the week, and in some cases it's the church that's to blame! Designing programs that divide and separate rather than unify and integrate is unproductive in the long run. Love makes every effort to bring people together rather than isolating them or pulling them apart from one another. There are plenty of ways to make teenagers and children feel special, but always isolating them from the body is unwise.

■ *"Evangelism, missions, outreach are the top priority,"* some say. We can set great goals for starting new congregations and missions ventures, but we better be sure the existing ones are not quietly dying due to neglect and lack of nurturing. While evangelism and outreach are certainly incredibly important to the life and future of a church, I have to wonder where we are going to bring the lost once they are saved? I hope we are bringing them back to a loving church family who will nurture, disciple, and minister to them as brothers and sisters in Christ. If not, they won't stay long despite our best efforts. They will eventually be attracted to a more loving, caring congregation where they can thrive and serve and grow.

Where We're Headed

Above all, continue to love each other deeply, because love covers a multitude of sins. Show hospitality to one another without complaining. As good managers of God's grace in its various forms, serve one another with the gift each of you has received.
—1 Peter 4:8–10 (ISV)

I don't want to dwell on the negative, but we seriously have to face the truth. And I know that there's hope for us as the people of God. I have seen a church member buy and repair a used car at his own expense and give it to a family in need with no strings attached. I know a church family that gave their Christmas money to missions rather than spending it on one another. There are thousands of churches who organize missions trips each year at their own expense to share the gospel with strangers in other countries or to do work projects for churches in impoverished areas locally or overseas. My father used to say quite often, "God's people are the best people in the

"God's people are the best people in the world!"

world!" and I know why. I have spent time with God's people in many countries and found them caring, loving, generous, kind, and servant-hearted.

In the coming chapters we will look at the character of God as He expressed Himself through love to His people. Then we'll learn how He commands us to do the same. We will see the difference between churches that understand the necessity of loving one another and those churches that have allowed other things to replace love in their midst. We are also going to look at what Christ expects of His people if they truly want to follow Him as His church. And we want to look at some prescriptions for what to do in a church that has lost its love. My ultimate goal in this book is to encourage God's people to look at love in a fresh way, as Christ intended us to view it, so that the world around us will be able to truly see the real meaning of love and be drawn to Christ through us.

> *Therefore if there is any consolation in Christ, if any comfort of love, if any fellowship of the Spirit, if any affection and mercy, fulfill my joy by being like-minded, having the same love, being of one accord, of one mind. Let nothing be done through selfish ambition or conceit, but in lowliness of mind let each esteem others better than himself. Let each of you look out not only for his own interests, but also for the interests of others.*
> —Philippians 2:1–4

To frame my perspective, I would like to propose the following recommendations to bring love back into our churches. You will find these elements incorporated throughout the book.

Simple Steps to Revive Love in the Church

STUDY CHRIST. If you want to know how to act as a person and as a church, go back and study the life of Christ and notice how He treated those whom God put in His pathway. Let Christ be your example of what practical and sacrificial love looks like and commit to imitating Him. Notice how he cared for the rich, the adulterer, the widows, the children, the religious leaders, and even those who crucified Him, and then do the same.

STUDY THE FIRST CHURCHES. The first churches were great examples of what love can look like among God's people. Unfortunately, we are more likely to compare ourselves to the church down the street than to the churches in the New Testament. Take time to notice Paul's exhortations to the churches he planted, and the way the church in Jerusalem began with prayer, fellowship, taking care of each other's needs, and true worship.

RESIST BLAMING AND JUDGING PEOPLE. Blaming and judging are passive behaviors that ask nothing of you except your opinion. Struggling people need more than your opinion, they need your involvement. Rather than expecting people to "just get more involved," or encouraging them to "just try to fit in," ask yourself what *you* should be doing personally to show other people the love of God whether they "deserve" it or not.

LOVE AS YOU WANT TO BE LOVED. Christ said we are to love others as we love ourselves. Would you like someone to drop off a meal to your home for your family when you are sick? Do that for others. Would you like someone to pray with you when you lose a loved one? Do that with someone else. Would you like someone to stop by your home to encourage you when you are lonely or depressed? Then do that for someone else. If you ever wonder if you should do something or get involved, the answer is a resounding yes! Better to do something, even if it may not seem needed, than to do nothing and miss a chance to be a tremendous blessing to someone in need. If you decide *not* to get involved because you "don't want to impose," then you have chosen to be unloving towards that person.

PRAY. Ask God what is on His heart for His people to do to show love to others. When you pray and seek the Lord, He will open your eyes and guide you with His Spirit to move you to action. Do not pray this prayer if you are not planning to be obedient to what He shows you. This would be grieving the Holy Spirit, and that is unwise. Pray also for others in need, especially if you are not personally able to do anything else to help them. That is an act of love.

JUST ASK. The only way you are ever going to know how to love people you don't know is to get to know them! Interview, or maybe even take to lunch, people in your church or community when you are unclear as to how to love them or help them in practical ways. Ask them what they need most. Make plans to help in the best ways you are able.

SURVEY YOUR CONGREGATION. Find out just how many people are present who are divorced, single parents, who have mental illnesses, who are fatherless, etc., and let God guide you to begin taking positive steps to help you love them in a practical and meaningful way.

LOOK OVER THE FENCE. See what other churches do to show love to various groups within their congregations.

Many churches are doing great things to minister and care for various groups of people in their community. There are great ministries to special-needs children, single moms, the divorced, the homeless, etc., that can be modified and incorporated into your own church ministry portfolio.

EQUIP PEOPLE TO LOVE. Many people use the excuse that they just don't know what to do. You can overcome this excuse by finding an individual or organization to offer training that sensitizes those in your church to the needs of others and equips them to do something about it. When you start to look for people to love, you will find them everywhere! Training opens people's eyes and gives them the skills and confidence to do something practical for those in need.

REPENT. If you realize after reading this book that your church has been withholding love from those God has been sending you, ask Him for forgiveness. Ask forgiveness from those who left your church because they felt unloved.

SHOW HOSPITALITY. Let your own home be a place where people experience the love of God without any pretensions, expectations, or strings attached. This will have a tremendous impact on your family and inspire them to notice those around them more often.

DO SOMETHING PRACTICAL. Doing something, anything, is *always* better than doing nothing at all! Anything you can do to show kindness and love to others is well worth doing.

■ ■ ■

The earthly life of Christ is truly a love story
from beginning to end.

■ ■ ■

Chapter 2

Love Demonstrated

The earthly life of Christ is truly a love story from beginning to end, and everything Christ did in between was motivated by love. If you want to be a loving person and have a loving church, there is no better way to begin than to study the One who best demonstrated love throughout His life.

There are many stories that show various aspects of His love towards people. For example, when Christ fed more than 5,000 people with loaves and fishes after giving them a five-course meal of spiritual food, He demonstrated that caring for the physical needs of people is an act of love. The Bible records this type of event on more than one occasion (Mark 6:30–44; 8:1–10, 19–21). There is no question that Christ had compassion on the multitudes, whose needs could be quite overwhelming at times. But His love is also seen through His encounters with individuals and smaller groups of people He encountered along the way.

Love Shows Mercy

Then the scribes and Pharisees brought to Him a woman caught in adultery. And when they had set her in the midst, they said to Him, "Teacher, this woman was caught in adultery, in the very act. Now Moses, in the law, commanded us that such should be stoned. But what do You say?" This they said, testing Him, that they might have something of which to accuse Him. But Jesus stooped down and wrote on the ground with His finger, as though He did not hear.
—John 8:3–6

When an adulterous woman was brought to Christ for judgment, He had the immediate challenge of deciding between the law and grace, between judgment and love, and between righteousness and mercy. The woman's accusers rightly pointed out that according to the law, her behavior warranted death. I don't want us to get distracted by side issues, but I am pretty sure there should have been a man there too as well, since, as the saying goes, "it takes two to tango," and the law also required the man to face punishment.

In certain countries today, a woman can be severely beaten or whipped simply for walking in public with a man who is not her husband. The situation confronting Jesus was far more serious. The laws against committing adultery were clear and in place for a reason. She was caught; no one questioned her guilt. The men surrounding her probably already had stones in their hands, because the verdict was unavoidable. She knew the penalty for her sin, she was old enough to choose right from wrong, and she chose what was wrong. She had to face the consequences for her sin. Her death would be upon her own head.

A decision had to be made, and these men would not leave without one. The law or grace? Righteousness or mercy? Condemnation or forgiveness? What I find absolutely astonishing about Christ's response is that He didn't actually choose between any of these, and further, He did not excuse the woman's behavior or sweep it under the carpet either. He actually acknowledged the woman's sin, but then demonstrated incredible love and compassion towards her. He demonstrated for us how it is possible to condemn a person's sin without condemning the person! He also prevented unwarranted violence against her and gave her a second chance. It has been said grace gives us what we don't deserve and mercy withholds what we do deserve. I believe in this situation Christ offered the woman both grace (a second chance) and mercy (sparing her the punishment of death she deserved).

> *So when they continued asking Him, He raised Himself up and said to them, "He who is without sin among you, let him throw a stone at her first." And again He stooped down and wrote on the ground. Then those who heard it, being convicted by their conscience, went out one by one, beginning with the oldest even to the last. And Jesus was left alone, and the woman standing in the midst.*
> —John 8:7–9

Do you realize what Jesus just did? His love even extended to the accusers. He knew they were intent on perpetrating an act of violence on this woman. They were going to needlessly take her life. Her blood would be upon their heads, because their hearts were not right before God. They had no compassion or concern whatsoever for her well-being. They saw in her merely a cynical opportunity to bring an accusation against Christ—even if she were killed in the process. Jesus created a way for them to realize exactly what they were doing, and save face. He could have done to them what they had just done to the woman and accused them of hypocrisy, judged the wickedness in their hearts, and sentenced them to God's punishment as well. But He didn't. He showed love even to these wicked, hard-hearted, self-righteous men.

He showed love even to these wicked, hard-hearted, self-righteous men.

Look also at the manner in which He spoke to the woman. He knelt down rather than lording His position over her as the other men were doing. He made Himself appear very vulnerable and non-threatening. He did not make eye contact with her but stared at the ground and wrote in the sand with His finger.

Other people may have immediately reacted emotionally, become defensive, or gone on the attack. But Jesus was likely breathing a prayer to His heavenly Father asking for wisdom and guidance. His meek behavior diffused the hostility and allowed for emotions to subside. He did not shame her or mock her or add to her guilt. He did not make her grovel or beg or plead for mercy. By the way, He had every right to do these things—to make her beg and grovel and plead for her life, for He was the only One present who was without sin, and therefore the only One who could have rightfully cast the first stone. Instead, He spoke quietly, rather than yelling or screaming at her for her obvious disregard of God's laws. And He gave her a second chance.

> *When Jesus had raised Himself up and saw no one but the woman, He said to her, "Woman, where are those accusers of yours? Has no one condemned you?" She said, "No one, Lord." And Jesus said to her, "Neither do I condemn you; go and sin no more."*
> —John 8:10–11

Christ did not overlook her sin. He did not look the other way in the face of her sin, for that would have been sin and committing that sin alone would have been enough to hang Him on the Cross. No, He forgave her sin as the only One who has that right. There is an enormous difference. And then the Good Doctor gave the woman a prescription for restoring her marriage and her life: "Go and sin no more." She had been searching for love in the wrong places, but in Christ she saw true love demonstrated for the first time.

Experiencing God's Love in the Church

Love Reveals Truth

Another troubled woman was drawing water from a well in the region of Samaria. It was a hot afternoon, and Jesus was thirsty. Going against several cultural norms, Jesus asked her for a drink of water. Even the woman herself was surprised: *"Then the woman of Samaria said to Him, 'How is it that You, being a Jew, ask a drink of me, a Samaritan woman?' For Jews have no dealings with Samaritans"* (John 4:9). We don't actually know if Jesus ever got His drink of water that day, but I don't believe that was His intention in the first place. Perhaps, when she left her bucket at the well and ran to bring the villagers to meet Jesus, He took a sip of water knowing He was about to spend the rest of the day talking to her neighbors!

Jesus knew the woman had a troubled past. She had been involved in a string of failed marriages, and it appears she had given marriage up altogether, as she now was living with a man to whom she was not married. Jesus intrigues her with truth: *"Jesus answered and said to her, 'Whoever drinks of this water will thirst again, but whoever drinks of the water that I shall give him will never thirst. But the water that I shall give him will become in him a fountain of water springing up into everlasting life.'"* (John 4:13–14).

She becomes curious. *"The woman said to Him, 'Sir, give me this water, that I may not thirst, nor come here to draw'"* (John 4:15).

Then Jesus begins to get to the heart of the matter, because she had been searching for love all of her life and could not find it. *"Jesus said to her, 'Go, call your husband, and come here.' The woman answered and said, 'I have no husband.' Jesus said to her, 'You have well said, "I have no husband," for you have had five husbands, and the one whom you now have is not your husband; in that you spoke truly.' The woman said to Him, 'Sir, I perceive that You are a prophet'"* (John 4:16–19).

Did you notice how Jesus again did not condemn the woman for her obvious problems with relationships, but offered her a second chance? He did not gloss over the truth of her sin, but addressed it head on, almost matter-of-factly. There must have been something in the tone of Jesus' voice that did not cause her to react defensively, as often happens when people perceive others are judging them. Not only was she not offended, she was intrigued—almost happy, it seems—that she had met a prophet. She engages Him with probably the only theological question she knew, and Jesus again shares with her truth about how to worship His Father. But the biggest truth was yet to come.

"The woman said to Him, 'I know that Messiah is coming' (who is called Christ). 'When He comes, He will tell us all things.' Jesus said to her, 'I who speak to you am He'" (John 4:25–26). How amazing it is that Christ would reveal to a troubled woman His true identity when He had kept it hidden from so many others!

This remarkable story shows how love can deal with the reality of sin in a way that brings life rather than condemnation and separation. It would have been unloving for Christ to walk on past her and go with the disciples into town. It would have been unloving for Christ to not try to address the deep needs in her troubled heart. It would have been unloving for Christ to leave her in her sin and not offer her a second chance at life and happiness. She had been searching for love all of her life and had one failure after another. Now love was searching for her and found her at the town well.

As Paul wrote to the believers in Ephesus, they, *"speaking the truth in love, may grow up in all things into Him who is the head—Christ"* (Ephesians 4:15). Christ is the Master of speaking the truth in love, and as we also learn to speak the truth in love to others we honor Him. Showing others love can be very difficult at times, but that never stopped our Lord.

Let me share a personal story with you. I have to admit I was a bit nervous as Mike Johnson drove me to his place of work. It was the men's shelter of Seattle's Union Gospel Mission, in Seattle's original downtown—the old brick Pioneer Square district. I had just finished a weekend retreat with the executive leaders and had some time before my flight departed, so I agreed to see where the frontline people in UGM worked. Having had no more interaction with "street people" than most people have in any given week, the alarm on my personal safety radar began to go off as I entered their world. I checked where my wallet and keys were and put on a brave-but-confident face as we parked the car and entered the building.

I think I now saw the homeless for the first time as individuals in need.

In some ways, I felt like Saul after his conversion, being brought by Barnabas to the church in Jerusalem—I needed a gatekeeper, one who knew the ropes and the people. Mike was the man. As we visited each of the four floors, I don't think there was a single person he saw to whom he did not give a bear hug. You should have seen the huge smiles. You should have seen the variety of toothless grins! I felt ashamed of my wariness as I began to see what love can do for those who are at the desperate end of their ropes. Computer training, resume writing, skills development, hot food, safe living quarters, Bible study, and worship were liberally offered to whomever would come and enter their programs.

I have rarely seen such a sense of fulfillment in one's work as I saw that day on Mike's face. He beamed as he told story after story of how people came to the Mission in desperate circumstances and were now working in jobs and putting their broken family relationships back together following years of neglect. I think I now saw the homeless for the first time as individuals in need. I also realized that it would not take very much for any one of us to end up in dire straits, in need of someone to show us the love of God in practical ways.

Love Disregards Critics

Jesus was never concerned about people's opinions of Him. He only really cared about the opinion His Father had of

Him. On several occasions, God let it be known, *"This is My beloved Son, in whom I am well pleased"* (Matthew 3:17, 7:5; 2 Peter 1:17). So when He was severely criticized for going to dinner with Matthew the tax collector and his tax collector friends (Matthew 9:10), He wasn't bothered. Nor was He particularly disturbed when people questioned His character and reputation after He chose to dine with Zacchaeus, the chief tax collector for all of Jericho (Luke 19:7). It didn't matter to Jesus whether the person was a troubled woman, a destitute widow, a wealthy ruler, or a known sinner; His love compelled Him to do what it took to change their hearts and lives.

Perhaps the religious rulers thought Jesus was on Zacchaeus's payroll, or that maybe this rich man had bought a miracle from the Good Teacher. In any case, they must have thought, Jesus *had* to be in league with sinners if He would actually go into one of their homes. But the results of Christ's visit were indisputable. In fact, many people in Jericho soon after experienced a noticeable economic upturn. Zacchaeus gave away half of all his ill-gotten wealth to the poor, and he gave back to everyone he had cheated four times what he had stolen from them.

The love of Christ changes hearts. Had Jesus been worried about what the people of Jericho would say if He dined with their chief tax collector, many of those very critics would have been denied their financial windfall. Had Jesus let His critics determine His agenda, the tax-gathering system would never have been reformed from the top down! Everyone in Jericho benefitted that day because love trumped the critics.

On several occasions, even Jesus' own disciples rebuked Him. Judas was shocked that He would allow a woman to waste expensive ointment by pouring it on Jesus' feet and told Jesus as much (John 12:4–5). Peter rebuked Jesus for saying He would be going to the Cross (Mark 8:32). Even His good friends Mary and Martha criticized Him for not coming in time to save their brother Lazarus from dying (John 11:21). But Christ's critics never deterred Him from doing what love does—freeing people from bondage, giving them second chances, addressing their

Experiencing God's Love in the Church

needs, and revealing truth to them. For Christ, demonstrating love was far more important than people's opinions or agendas for Him.

Love Notices the Small Things

There are a few accounts from our Lord's life that frankly amaze me. It is not the miracles that grab my attention, it is the attention to detail that Christ showed. Not administrative details, or organizational details, but people details. Notice what Jesus notices.

As Jesus sat facing the Temple offering box, he watched how individuals dropped their money into it. Many rich people were dropping in large amounts, probably creating quite a stir. Then a destitute widow came and dropped in two small copper coins, worth about a cent. I doubt they even made a sound as they slid down the chute. He called His disciples and said to them, *"Assuredly, I say to you that this poor widow has put in more than all those who have given to the treasury; for they all put in out of their abundance, but she out of her poverty put in all that she had, her whole livelihood"* (Mark 12:43–44).

Not only did Christ see what everyone else missed, but He chose to point it out as an example of the kind of heart that pleases Him. Clearly, Christ greatly valued what others saw as insignificant. This woman was neglected by society and wholly dependent upon God for her survival. She had nothing to offer God but the little she had left. Christ did not point out the wealthy or influential for their generous gifts, but the poor widow who most would have considered a burden on society. As she privately gave God her last coins, Christ publicly honors her. The next story is similar:

And when Jesus was in Bethany at the house of Simon the leper, a woman came to Him having an alabaster flask of very costly fragrant oil, and she poured it on His head as He sat at the table. But when His disciples saw it,

they were indignant, saying, "Why this waste? For this fragrant oil might have been sold for much and given to the poor." But when Jesus was aware of it, He said to them, "Why do you trouble the woman? For she has done a good work for Me. For you have the poor with you always, but Me you do not have always. For in pouring this fragrant oil on My body, she did it for My burial. Assuredly, I say to you, wherever this gospel is preached in the whole world, what this woman has done will also be told as a memorial to her."
—Matthew 26:6–13

Mark 14:4–5 says the disciples actually became very angry with this woman. Christ honors her first by not embarrassing her as His disciples did, and second, by making sure every person who reads the Bible knows about her act of devotion to Him. Something that was done in private, an act of personal devotion and love, has been preserved and is now an example for all of us of what sacrificial worship should look like. Christ's values are so different from most people's values. If we are to truly serve Him, we need to value what He values.

Love Is Moved by Compassion

Time and time again Christ is moved by compassion on others: two blind men (Matthew 20:34), hungry crowds (Matthew 9:36), a lone leper (Mark 1:41)—and in some cases He gave people back their very lives in more ways than one.

As he approached the entrance to the city, a man who had died was being carried out. He was his mother's only son, and she was a widow. A large crowd from the city was with her. When the Lord saw her, he felt compassion for her. He said to her, "You can stop crying." Then he went up and touched the bier, and the men who were carrying it stopped. He said, "Young man, I say to you,

*get up!" The man who had been dead sat up and began
to speak, and Jesus gave him back to his mother.*
—Luke 7:12–15 (ISV)

Compassion means to have pity on someone, or to be moved deeply because of a person's situation. Jesus could have walked on by. After all, lots of people die at an early age. But something about the woman moved Christ's heart to action. Her last surviving family member was now gone and she had no one to care for her. Her heart was broken, her future was precarious. But now the one Person who could actually do something about it happened to be walking by at just the right moment. Up to now, Jesus had not raised anyone from the dead. But it was on behalf of a distraught mother that Christ chose to reveal the extent of His miracle-working powers.

> **It is easy to walk on by people in need, but Jesus was moved to action by His love for people.**

It is easy to walk on by people in need, but Jesus was moved to action by His love for people. It is a dangerous place to be when we no longer feel compassion for others or no longer feel sympathetic to their needs. I hear unthinking people comment how lazy the poor must be, or that their dire circumstance is their own fault. Christ was righteous through and through. True righteousness, it seems, means getting involved in the messy lives of others. A prostitute, a woman caught in adultery, a demon-possessed man, a leper, a woman who was bleeding, a man who terrorized the Christian community, and other outcasts of society were the ones Christ seemed drawn to the most. Everyone was on Christ's visitation list. No one was too far gone to receive mercy, compassion, or love.

Love Does the Hard Things

There are times when love has to say the hard things. To ignore sin, to turn a blind eye to injustice, and to overlook

Love is not just warm fuzzy feelings, commitment, and loyalty.

"indiscretions" essentially shows a lack of love. As a parent, I would speak out if my child was about to make a terrible mistake. I would object to my son's or daughter's choices if I knew they were not honoring to God. I would levy any force I could to stop them if I thought they were going to do something harmful to themselves or to others. We are God's children. He loves us as a parent loves a child. In fact, the Bible tells us that like a good father, our heavenly Father actually disciplines those He loves. The writer of Hebrews tells us:

> *You have forgotten the encouragement that is addressed to you as sons: "My son, do not think lightly of the Lord's discipline or give up when you are corrected by him. For the Lord disciplines the one he loves, and he punishes every son he accepts." What you endure disciplines you: God is treating you as sons. Is there a son whom his father does not discipline? Now if you are without any discipline, in which all sons share, then you are illegitimate and not God's sons. Furthermore, we had earthly fathers who disciplined us, and we respected them for it. We should submit even more to the Father of our spirits and live, shouldn't we?*
> —Hebrews 12:5–9 (ISV)

Christ's love included offering discipline to those who required it. Love is not just warm fuzzy feelings, commitment, and loyalty. It also includes doing the difficult things out of concern for others and for their own best interests whether they like it or not. This kind of love needs to be God-directed and pursued only after much prayer to be sure your motives are pure and your actions are truly loving.

Love Is Not Afraid to Confront Wrongs

At first glance Matthew 23 may appear out of place when talking about love, but it perfectly illustrates my point about love doing the hard things. In this passage it is as though Jesus unloads both barrels on the religious leaders of the day. He'd had enough of their criticism; their plotting; their proud, arrogant hearts; their posturing; and their abuse of His people who were like sheep being pillaged by wolves. The following remarks seem out of place for a man full of grace and compassion:

- *"So do whatever they tell you and follow it, but stop doing what they do, because they don't do what they say."*—Matthew 23:3 (ISV)

- *"They do everything to be seen by people."*—Matthew 23:5 (ISV)

- *"How terrible it will be for you, scribes and Pharisees, you hypocrites!"*—Matthew 23:13 (ISV)

- *"How terrible it will be for you, blind guides!"*—Matthew 23:16 (ISV)

- *"You blind fools!"*—Matthew 23:17 (ISV)

- *"You blind men!"*—Matthew 23:19 (ISV)

- *"You blind Pharisee!"*—Matthew 23:26 (ISV)

- *"How terrible it will be for you, scribes and Pharisees, you hypocrites! You are like whitewashed tombs that look beautiful on the outside but inside are full of dead people's bones and every kind of impurity."*—Matthew 23:27 (ISV)

> ■ *You snakes, you children of serpents! How can you escape being condemned to hell?*
> —Matthew 23:33 (ISV)

Serious stuff! Jesus doesn't mince His words here; He tells them exactly what He thinks of them. This seems so foreign to church culture today, where we much prefer to talk about people behind their backs instead of to their faces! So how does this square with loving others?

Jesus gives a demonstration of love in its most challenging form—daring to tell the truth, daring to say what needs to be said, and daring to confront those who need to be confronted. Jesus was certainly not concerned with hurting their feelings, particularly those who should know better. These were powerful and influential leaders. Jesus confronted strength with strength. No one intimidated these people. They set the rules and they abused the rules they set. Everyone in the community was aware of this. It was no secret that there was corruption among the religious leaders. They were arrogant and proud. They were hypocritical and abusers of power. Jesus was only saying what everyone was thinking but did not have the fortitude to say.

Jesus gives a demonstration of love in its most challenging form—daring to tell the truth.

No wonder the religious leaders wanted to silence Christ; He was messing up a good thing. He was holding them accountable, something no one else could do. You see, there was an unwritten understanding between the Roman government and the Jewish leaders, sort of a turn-the-blind-eye relationship. The common person was caught between a ruthless government and corrupt leaders. Everyone was doing what was right in his own eyes and ignoring God's standards—everyone, that is, except Jesus.

Yes, He loved the religious leaders; He was going to be crucified for them too. But He could not stand by and let them continue in their offenses. Like any loving parent, He loved His children enough to tell them the truth, to point out God's expectations, and to give them a warning of what was coming if they did not change their evil and corrupt ways.

I remember a young man coming to me asking for prayer. The relationship between him and his girlfriend was strained, and their son was an unwilling witness to an increasing amount of domestic disputes. This man had not married his son's mother. She knew there was no real commitment for him to stick around if times got tough. I told him that the problem was not so much between him and his girlfriend, but between him and his God. I shared with him that once he made things right with God and was living a life that followed God's principles, things would improve with his girlfriend. I was able to provide premarital counseling and perform their marriage a few months later. They now have several children together and are serving the Lord in their local church. The challenge was not to point a critical or condemning finger at him, but through love, to show him a better way.

Love Is Unfeigned

Let love be without hypocrisy. Abhor what is evil. Cling to what is good. Be kindly affectionate to one another with brotherly love, in honor giving preference to one another.
—Romans 12:9–10

We give no offense in anything, that our ministry may not be blamed. But in all things we commend ourselves as ministers of God: in much patience, in tribulations, in needs, in distresses, in stripes, in imprisonments, in tumults, in labors, in sleeplessness, in fastings; by purity, by knowledge, by longsuffering, by kindness, by the Holy Spirit, by sincere love.
—2 Corinthians 6:3–6

Sincere means without hypocrisy, unfeigned. There are no ulterior motives, just a desire to do what is in the best interest of others. I have been asked, "How exactly are we to love our enemies?" I tell people that we are to wish our enemies only God's best. We don't have to like them, but we have to love them, or wish them what God wants them to have, whether they want it or not. Now God's best for them may include discipline or judgment, but it may also include blessing. We'll leave that up to Him!

Christ had a purpose to fulfill while He tarried on earth. His mission was to bring the good news of salvation, to set people free from bondage, to heal the brokenhearted, and to embody the Father's love for His people. So everything He said and everything He did was intended as a way to demonstrate that love.

There's a great deal of self-confidence required to show love to others this way. In fact, the stronger and more powerful you are, the more self-control you need in order to be gentle. The Bible tells us that everything was created through Christ. He was the One who calmed the raging seas with a word, who raised the dead with a word, who set people free from Satan's bondage with a word. And yet...

- Imagine Jesus Christ, the Son of God, the Creator of the universe, the King of kings and Lord of lords quietly stooping down to the ground before an adulterous woman caught in sin.

- Imagine Jesus ignoring the tut-tutting of Jericho's religious leaders and going to lunch with Zacchaeus, one of the most hated men in the city.

- Imagine the Christ of God carefully putting a small child on His knee to teach His disciples a lesson about humility.

■ Imagine Him letting a notoriously sinful woman wash His feet with her tears and dry them with her hair. (That's a lot of tears, folks. I have to wonder if this was the same woman caught in adultery whom He had earlier forgiven.)

In one of the most revealing passages of Scripture, John 17, Jesus shows us His heart for His disciples as He prays to His Father just prior to His arrest and crucifixion. In what has been called the "high priestly prayer," Christ ends by saying:

"I have given them the glory that you gave me, so that they may be one, just as we are one. I am in them, and you are in me. May they be completely one, so that the world may know that you sent me and that you have loved them as you loved me. Father, I want those you have given me to be with me where I am and to see my glory, which you gave me because you loved me before the creation of the world. Righteous Father, the world has never known you. Yet I have known you, and these men have known that you sent me. I made your name known to them, and will continue to make it known, so that the love you have for me may be in them and I myself may be in them."
—John 17:22–26 (ISV)

In some ways, all that Christ did on earth came down to this one last statement: His life's purpose, His sacrifice, the miracles He did, the teachings, and the price He paid were all intended to demonstrate God's love for us, and, as a result of His love in us, we should go and do likewise. When we sometimes think God is being too harsh or judgmental, or that He is somehow not being fair with us, we simply have to look to the Cross and remember the costly sacrifice He paid for our sin—because He loved us.

■ ■ ■

I believe Christ is expecting the church
to look even better with age!

■ ■ ■

Chapter 3

Love as God Intended

Husbands, love your wives, just as Christ also loved the church and gave Himself for her, that He might sanctify and cleanse her with the washing of water by the word, that He might present her to Himself a glorious church, not having spot or wrinkle or any such thing, but that she should be holy and without blemish.
—Ephesians 5:25–27

Knowing that Christ "gave Himself up" for the church and purchased it with His own blood (Acts 20:28), we should not be surprised that Christ has certain expectations for His church. The One who sacrificed His own life for the church expects the church to continue to function as He intended it to function until His return. Paul compares the love a husband has for his wife to the love Christ has for His church and explains that Christ will one day return for His bride, hoping to find her in pretty good shape. In fact, I believe Christ is expecting the church to look even better with age!

The truth is, what Jesus Christ expects of His church is no different from what He expects from each person who calls Him "Lord." The focus is the same, the objectives are the same, the character is the same, and the priorities and behaviors should also be the same. Each person is an extension of Christ's body, the church. In a spiritual sense Christ and His body, the church, are one, and He does not act independently from His body, though many individual Christians may try to live that way.

What Does Christ Expect?

First and foremost, Christ expects that those who address Him as Lord will love Him in response to the sacrificial love He demonstrated for them by dying on the Cross in their place. We should always respond in love to our Creator. Love brings together the human and the divine. John writes, *"We love Him because He first loved us"* (1 John 4:19). It is only out of our love for Christ that we can even contemplate living a life worthy of Him who died for us. It is out of love that we would give up things we really don't need in order to gain that which we could never have apart from Christ. It should be out of our love for Christ that we meet and study together, sing worship and praise songs, give our money, and seek to share the gospel with others.

But love is a challenging word to define. Is it simple devotion or loyalty? Yes. Will it involve sacrifice? Yes. Strong feelings and affections? Yes. Fellowship? Yes. Can it bring both deep pain and great joy? Yes. Love is all of these things and much more. When Christ called His followers to love, He had in mind the kind of love He demonstrated towards us—selfless and sacrificial. It is described in Paul's letter to the believers in Corinth. His definition of love looks like this:

■ *Love is patient and kind;*

■ *It is not jealous or conceited or proud;*

- *Love is not ill-mannered or selfish or irritable; love does not keep a record of wrongs;*

- *Love is not happy with evil, but is happy with the truth.*

- *Love never gives up; and its faith, hope, and patience never fail.*

- *Love is eternal.*
  —1 Corinthians 13:4–6 (GNT)

Christ actually defined what love is and demonstrated for us the lengths to which love will go. God the Son modeled for us the fact that God is love (1 John 4:8). What many people fail to realize is that Christ's life and actions are not just to be admired or respected, they are a model and an example He deliberately left for us to follow. *"This is how we know what love is: Christ gave his life for us. We too, then, ought to give our lives for our brothers and sisters!"* (1 John 3:16 GNT).

God the Son modeled for us the fact that God is love.

Love is more than just a feeling; it *always* leads to action. *"God so loved the world that he gave His only begotten Son"* (John 3:16). *"But God demonstrates His own love toward us, in that while we were still sinners, Christ died for us"* (Romans 5:8). We can say we love God, but it is in our actions that we prove we love God. What Christ wants to see in His followers, in His church, is a demonstration of love in action as opposed to merely just saying words or singing songs about love.

Loving Him Through Obedience

Christ said, *"If you love Me, keep My commandments"* (John 14:15). John writes, *"For this is the love of God, that we keep His commandments, and His commandments are not burdensome"* (1 John 5:3). This means the one thing the church can do to demonstrate love for Christ is to obey simply and wholeheartedly what He taught us to do. Of course that presupposes that the people in the church actually know what Christ commanded. For example, Christ commanded that we not be above serving one another even in the most menial way, if there is a need. There can be no one who is above serving even the "least" of those. As we serve others who appear to be the least important in the eyes of the world, we are acting out our love for Christ.

Love for God.

"Jesus said to him, 'You shall love the Lord your God with all your heart, with all your soul, and with all your mind'" (Matthew 22:37). If we are able to love God, it demonstrates that the love of God is in us, for *"everyone who loves is born of God and knows God"* (1 John 4:7). You might think that loving the One who demonstrated such amazing love toward us should be a given, fairly straightforward and easy to manage. But God is calling us to a passionate, sold-out, body-and-soul kind of love. Learning to love God like that takes a lifetime of walking with Him through the mountaintops and the valleys, the spiritual highs and the dry and barren times, the lean days and the times of abundance, and the many ordinary days in between. As we begin to grasp the foundational importance of loving God, Christ then expands the circle of love a little larger.

> **God is calling us to a passionate, sold-out, body-and-soul kind of love.**

Love for one another.

"This is My commandment, that you love one another as I have loved you" (John 15:12). This commandment was added to the existing commands, included with the Ten Commandments that

His Father had given many generations earlier in the Book of Deuteronomy. John includes this command of Christ four different times in his Gospel. Why was this so important to Christ? Because by loving one another, it shows outsiders that the followers of Christ are actually following Christ! Jesus said, *"By this all will know that you are My disciples, if you have love for one another"* (John 13:35). This is the one indicator that a person is truly a Christian; it's not just if they have a love for God in heaven, but if they love their fellow Christians here on earth. To be a Christian is to exhibit Christ's love within the church (toward His brothers and sisters). By implication, the opposite is also true: if a person is unable to love his or her fellow Christians, it is a good bet that the love of Christ is not in that person. Here's Christ's expectation in this regard: *"As I have loved you ... you also love one another"* (John 13:34). Again, Christ commanded His people to follow His example of what it means to love. So we see that love is not only spiritual, it is also practical. And as we see the necessity of loving God and our fellow Christians, Christ expands the circle wider still.

So we see that love is not only spiritual, it is also practical.

Love for our neighbors.

"You shall love your neighbor as yourself" (Matthew 22:39). A man seeking a little more explanation on this command approached Jesus for clarification (Luke 10:29). He wanted to know who actually qualified to be his neighbor. So Christ tells the famous story of the Good Samaritan. The victim in His story—most likely a Jew—traveled from Jerusalem in the hill country down to Jericho, located near the Dead Sea. After he was attacked by robbers, the only person to help him was a Samaritan. To the Jews, Samaritans were social outcasts and objects of hate. For Christ to make a Samaritan the hero of His story was more than a little offensive to His listeners. Yet when Jesus

asked them who it was who demonstrated mercy, who acted as a neighbor, they had to admit it was the Samaritan—and not the religious Jews. Then Christ said to the questioner, in effect, "Go and be like a good Samaritan!"

You see, in the kingdom of God, there are no boundaries to love. Christ died for the just and the unjust, for every man, woman, and child, no matter what their race, culture, or nationality. Just as God does not see one person as more deserving than another to receive His love, so we too should not deny anyone our love. But loving God, one another, and our neighbors is not the extent of our call; Christ further challenges us to draw the circle even larger.

Love for the unloving.

"Love your enemies, do good to those who hate you, bless those who curse you, and pray for those who spitefully use you" (Luke 6:27–28). Tough words! But remember, Christ willingly demonstrated for us what He expects His followers to do. Even at the very end of His life on earth, while nailed to a Roman cross, He demonstrated love for His enemies. In some of His very last words, Christ said, "Father, forgive them, for they do not know what they do" (Luke 23:34). Even while His abusers mocked and ridiculed Him and gambled for the clothes they had just stripped off His mutilated flesh, Christ showed compassion, grace, and love for them. Christ knew that Judas, one of His 12 closest companions, one with whom He spent the better part of three years, would betray Him for a bag of silver coins. Christ knew who His betrayer would be, and yet we have no indication that He treated him any differently than the other 11 disciples. Even though He knew Judas's heart was bent on evil, He still loved him. Jesus also knew that the other disciples would fail Him but, as John writes, "having loved His own who were in the world, He loved them to the end" (John 13:1). Christ's love went the distance.

Do you see how important love is to Christ? If it is so incredibly important to our Master, we, as His followers, should endeavour to demonstrate love to God, to one another, to those around us, and even to those who hate us. We cannot run from the fact that love should be the very fabric from which Christians are made. When the Bible tells us to *"put on Christ"* (Galatians 3:27; Romans 13:14), we should envision literally clothing ourselves with love.

Love in Action

Christ wants His people to live lives that demonstrate their love for Him by putting that love into action toward others, particularly the poor, the needy, and "the least of these." Remember what Christ said in Matthew's Gospel:

> **Demonstrating love for Christ means getting your hands dirty meeting the needs of others.**

"And He will set the sheep on His right hand, but the goats on the left. Then the King will say to those on His right hand, 'Come, you blessed of My Father, inherit the kingdom prepared for you from the foundation of the world: for I was hungry and you gave Me food; I was thirsty and you gave Me drink; I was a stranger and you took Me in; I was naked and you clothed Me; I was sick and you visited Me; I was in prison and you came to Me...Inasmuch as you did it to one of the least of these My brethren, you did it to Me."

"Then He will also say to those on the left hand, 'Depart from Me, you cursed, into the everlasting fire prepared for the devil and his angels...Assuredly, I say to you, inasmuch as you did not do it to one of the least of these, you did not do it to Me.' And these will go away into everlasting punishment, but the righteous into eternal life."
—Matthew 25:33–46

Demonstrating love for Christ is shown in meeting the practical needs of the disadvantaged, the new immigrant who needs to feel welcomed and connected, the sick and diseased, the homeless man and the AIDS orphan, the incarcerated criminal, and the struggling pastor. Demonstrating love for Christ means getting your hands dirty meeting the needs of others.

Amazing Love in Burundi

Freddy was born and grew up in Burundi and lived through the ethnic genocide that swept through his country and neighboring Rwanda in the 1990s. Freddy, a Christian, was a school teacher during the killings. One night eight students were killed in the school where he was teaching, and many of his boarding school students' families were murdered, leaving him as the only adult they trusted. Freddy knew he had to do more than pray for his country. He resigned as a teacher and started Youth for Christ in Burundi.

I met Freddy for the first time when he greeted me in the Bujumbura airport parking lot. After a day of speaking to young people in the capital, Freddy took me on a journey some two hours inland. The African mountains of Burundi from Bujumbura to Gitega are absolutely breathtaking, presenting amazing vistas in extreme contrast to the surrounding flatlands. Coffee bushes, banana trees, mangos, avocados, family farms, and villages left me wide-eyed and very much aware that I was in a world very different from the western coast of Canada.

Freddy took me to a complex that included a recently established and growing orphanage housing 31 children, a school, and a building waiting to be used as a medical clinic, all of which were started under Freddy's care. He had prayed for God to show him how to put action to his dream of training young people in the Lord who would in turn grow up and impact their country with godly morals and values. God moved in amazing ways: Incredibly, a Muslim man gave Freddy ten acres of land for free. God then brought other like-hearted people from Australia, Ireland, South Africa, the US, and Canada who were able to raise funding to build a secure compound with wonderful facilities to house and care for the orphans. God also gave him the means to design and construct a medical clinic where a nurse could provide for the physical needs of both the children and the community.

I was impacted by many things during my stay with him. I couldn't help notice that these small orphaned children were incredibly happy. Someone had shown them the love of God, and they radiated that love in return. Many had been abandoned, some had HIV/AIDS, and yet all were given a home and a family to replace the one they had lost. Through donations of caring people, these orphans are actually eating better than most of the people in the surrounding community. I can't help but think Jesus smiles when He looks at what Freddy is doing. Burundi needs more godly leaders like Freddy and his staff who will live out their faith and redeem a nation devastated by hate and conflict. True Christian love always leads to action.

Freddy is a very ordinary person who serves an extraordinary God. When Freddy asked God to show him how to demonstrate love for his country and his people, doors began to open. Anyone can take time and notice needs around them, but not everyone will take the time before God to find out what He has on His heart and mind to do to meet those needs.

God the Father, a God of Love

Jesus said, *"As the Father loved Me, I also have loved you; abide in My love"* (John 15:9).

In John 5:39-42, Christ teaches His disciples about their loving heavenly Father. The relationship Jesus has with His Father is the model for the kind of love relationship He wants to have with His disciples.

He tells them that *"The Son can do nothing of Himself, but what He sees the Father do; for whatever He does, the Son also does in like manner. For the Father loves the Son, and shows Him all things that He Himself does…I do not seek My own will but the will of the Father who sent Me"* (John 5:19–20, 30). Then He turned to those who were trying to trap Him and accuse Him, and accuses them of seeking eternal life apart from God's Messiah. In fact they refuse to believe Christ's revelation of who He is, so He ends with this indictment, *"But I know you, that you do not have the love of God in you"* (John 5:42).

Jesus' love for others was founded upon and emanated from His love relationship with His Father. So too, our love for others must emanate from our love relationship with Christ. The measure of the depth and strength of our relationship with Christ is shown in how we love one another.

Love is the recurring theme throughout Christ's ministry. We see Him looking at the mass of people gathering around Him clamoring for physical and spiritual nourishment. Matthew records, *"But when He saw the multitudes, He was moved with compassion for them, because they were weary and scattered, like sheep having no shepherd"* (Matthew 9:36). At another time, Christ came up to Jerusalem from Bethany, and, as He descended from the Mount of Olives to the city below, He was overcome with sorrow for His people who had rejected His love. *"Now as He drew near, He saw the city and wept over it, saying, 'If you had known, even you, especially in this your day, the things that make for your peace! But...You did not know the time of your visitation'"* (Luke 19:41–42, 44). He knew that in a few years the city would be besieged by the Roman army, the Temple and the walls would be destroyed, and many of the people slaughtered. Christ knew that it all could have been averted had the people simply returned to their loving and forgiving God, but they refused.

Christ expects that we will have the same heart as He has for people, that we will treat them in the same way as He would treat them: as though they are Christ Himself. Mother Teresa would always say that what motivated her to spend her life caring for the sick and the dying of Calcutta was the conviction that in serving them she was serving Jesus. When the Bible tells us that we are Christ's "body," the meaning is figurative, but the action is literal. In other words, Christ ascended to heaven to prepare a place for us, but He left us to continue the work He began in bringing hope, freedom, and love to a lost world. We know what is on His heart because He so often told us what is important to Him and to His Father. Time and time again the prophets tell us that God has a compassionate heart for the widow, the orphan, and the foreigner—those who had no legal recourse in society and who were often left to their own devices. The heart of Matthew 25, the story of the sheep and the goats, is reflected in a much earlier passage in the Old Testament:

> *"For the LORD your God is God of gods and Lord of lords, the great God, mighty and awesome, who shows no partiality nor takes a bribe. He administers justice for the fatherless and the widow, and loves the stranger, giving him food and clothing. Therefore love the stranger, for you were strangers in the land of Egypt."*
> —Deuteronomy 10:17–19

I hope you have noticed in your study of the Bible that the Father and the Son have the same heart! You also likely have noticed that the majority of Christ's public ministry was spent among the poor, the needy, the sick, and the common people. Only occasionally do we find Jesus sitting down to a meal with a religious leader (Luke 7:36) or conversing with those in the ruling class (Luke 18:18–19). He was more often accused of cavorting with sinners (Matthew 9:11; Luke 5:30).

By His own admission, Christ came to seek and to save that which was lost (Luke 19:10) and to act as a physician to those who were in need (Luke 5:31–32). The heart of our Lord and Master was always sympathetic to those who were in need. The fact of the matter is that the wealthy, the powerful, the influential, and the self-sufficient often do not feel that they are in need. Three of the four Gospels record Jesus saying, *"For it is easier for a camel to go through the eye of a needle than for a rich man to enter the kingdom of God"* (Luke 18:25; see also Matthew 19:24 and Mark 10:25).

Do You Love Me?

I don't mention orphans, the poor, and the needy to induce feelings of guilt, but rather to remind us that too often it is those with whom Christ spent the least amount of time that we too often try to spend the most amount of time. We obsess over wanting what the rich have—their cars, their houses, their vacations, their clothing, their jewelry, their influence—and many times neglect the very ones who were truly important to Christ. Too often we see people for what we can get from them rather than how we can serve them. As my wife has remarked, "Some people are placed in the body of Christ just to teach us how to love without expecting anything in return." Christ asked so little of His followers, but what He asked for was what was most important. Look at this exchange between Jesus and Peter after His resurrection:

> So when they had eaten breakfast, Jesus said to Simon Peter, "Simon, son of Jonah, do you love Me more than these?" He said to Him, "Yes, Lord; You know that I love You." He said to him, "Feed My lambs."
>
> He said to him again a second time, "Simon, son of Jonah, do you love Me?" He said to Him, "Yes, Lord; You know that I love You." He said to him, "Tend My sheep."
>
> He said to him the third time, "Simon, son of Jonah, do you love Me?" Peter was grieved because He said to him the third time, "Do you love Me?" And he said to Him, "Lord, You know all things; You know that I love You." Jesus said to him, "Feed My sheep."
> —John 21:15–17

Notice Jesus did not ask Peter whether he respected Him, or admired Him, or feared Him, or if he was willing to serve Him or even sacrifice much for Him. It was important to both Jesus and Peter to know once and for all whether or not Peter really loved Him. You see, Peter had professed to love Christ more than the rest of the disciples and even was willing to die for Him (Mark 14:29, 31). But only hours later, Peter vehemently denied even knowing Christ, not once but three times (John 18:15–18, 25–27). So three times Christ asks Peter to affirm his love for Him. When Christ addresses Peter in these verses, He does not call him Peter, or Cephas (the rock), but Simon son of Jonah, the name by which Peter was known before he became a disciple.

It was as though Jesus were taking Peter back to the beginning when they first met, just like the day Christ called him out of his fishing boat to follow Him. The Good Shepherd wanted to know whether or not He could truly count on Peter to care for His sheep and feed the tender lambs. For if Peter did not truly love Christ, the flock would be resented, neglected, and left abandoned. Christ wanted to ensure that Peter loved Him before He could entrust Peter to look after His flock. Notice the care with which Jesus speaks to Peter, allowing him to offer three affirmations of love to make up for the three denials. Notice also that Peter no longer pretends to love Christ more than the others and merely affirms that he truly does love Him. It was a humbling time for Peter and for all the other disciples, all of whom had abandoned Christ during His arrest. But it was a new day and a new opportunity to pledge their love and their loyalty to Him.

So what was on the heart of our Lord as He spoke to Peter?

We know that Jesus did not have a literal flock of sheep grazing nearby. So what was on the heart of our Lord as He spoke to Peter? Jesus knows that those who do not truly love Him will have no love either for the lost or for His people. He was shortly going to be with His Father in heaven, and it had been His plan all along to leave His disciples with the responsibility to continue His work and ministry. They were now going to be the examples new Christians would follow.

Are We Controlled by Love?

The Apostle Paul certainly knew Christ's love. Christ could have killed him on the road to Damascus for how ruthlessly Paul (then Saul) had treated Christians, but instead He chose to transform his heart and commission him as an apostle to the Gentiles. Paul was forever grateful and explained to the church in Corinth his motivation for serving the Lord: *"For the love of Christ compels us, because we judge thus: that if One died for all, then all died; and He died for all, that those who live should live no longer for themselves, but for Him who died for them and rose again"* (2 Corinthians 5:14–15).

"The love of Christ compels us." That is an intriguing phrase Paul uses. Other translations use the word *controls* or *constrains*. The Greek word translated here can mean being "held or pressed together" such as in a crowd or throng of people. It can also be used to mean being held as a prisoner, being afflicted by something, or even being preoccupied. It is often difficult to give the full range of meanings when translating a word into another language. I believe Paul likely intended to convey to the church in Corinth that they had no higher calling than to be ever mindful of Christ's love working through them.

And yet as I visit many different churches, my sense is that they have lost every inkling of the compelling love of Christ in their midst.

Loving Others *Is* Loving Christ

Celebrated Christian author Henri Nouwen became so overwhelmed with the notion of God's love that he sought to do something to demonstrate his unfettered love for God in return. He chose to give up his career as a sought-after professor and speaker at Menninger Foundation Clinic, University of Notre Dame, Yale University, and Harvard University to become a pastor for residents at the L'Arche community of Daybreak in Toronto, Canada. He lived in one of the homes and was asked to help Adam Arnett, a man with a severe disability, with his morning routine. Adam was not able to communicate his gratitude for the constant care that Nouwen provided him. He was barely able to acknowledge Nouwen's presence. Nouwen explained his motivation was to experience what it was like to render service to people without any expectation of thanks in return, only knowing that in doing so he was demonstrating his love for Christ. (You can read more in *Seeds of Hope: A Henri Nouwen Reader*).

I have to wonder: what exactly is it that Christ's love compels me to do? Or, do I feel any sense of compulsion whatsoever? Certainly a handful of men felt compelled enough to effectively change the world with the message of God's love. Christ's love transformed them from disciples to apostles as they took His message of love around the known world.

Jesus said, *"If you keep My commandments, you will abide in My love, just as I have kept My Father's commandments and abide in His love"* (John 15:10). He expects that we will "abide in Him." To abide primarily means to stay, as in describing the place you are located. It also means to continue, dwell, remain, and stand. Christ implores us to remain in the state of His love. Because love is not a physical location, we are able to be in His love constantly wherever we go and whatever we do. Just as you can be at peace whatever your circumstances, so too can we function from the standpoint of Christ's love at all times and in all places.

When we remain in Christ's love, or abide in Him, we are then able to fulfill other expectations:

- ■ *"To him who strikes you on the one cheek, offer the other also. And from him who takes away your cloak, do not withhold your tunic either.*

- ■ *"Give to everyone who asks of you. And from him who takes away your goods do not ask them back.*

■ *"And just as you want men to do to you, you also do to them likewise.*

■ *"But if you love those who love you, what credit is that to you? For even sinners love those who love them. And if you do good to those who do good to you, what credit is that to you? For even sinners do the same. And if you lend to those from whom you hope to receive back, what credit is that to you? For even sinners lend to sinners to receive as much back.*

■ *"But love your enemies, do good, and lend, hoping for nothing in return; and your reward will be great, and you will be sons of the Most High. For He is kind to the unthankful and evil."*
—Luke 6:29–35

The more we understand and appreciate the love Christ has for us, the more we will be able to demonstrate love to others. Jesus foreshadows the ultimate act of love when He says, *"Greater love has no one than this, than to lay down one's life for his friends"* (John 15:13). Sometimes when I speak to groups across the country, I will have them look at the people around them. Most will do as I ask. Then I ask them to do it once again, this time not looking at the person, but instead into that person's eyes. They do it, but this time with a nervous giggle. Then I say to them, "Until you are at the point that you are willing to die for those you have just looked at, you have not yet loved them as Christ expects us to."

Not every person is asked to lay down his or her life for his or her friends, but on occasion, there are situations where people have to make that decision. Patty Irby, a friend and long-time member of Wedgwood Baptist Church in Fort Worth, Texas, shared the following story with me.

On September 15, 1999, a concert was held at Wedgwood to celebrate the See You at the Pole events that had taken place at schools earlier in the day. There were several hundred young people in the auditorium for the concert, and there were youth groups from several churches. Larry Ashbrook entered the building from the south entrance and pulled out a gun. He shot and killed seven people, including four teens, and wounded seven others. He then killed himself.

Mary Beth Talley had been standing down the hallway at the CD table. When she heard the shots, she ran into the auditorium to warn others, but could not be heard over the music. The sister of one of Mary Beth's friends had come to the concert and was sitting on the back row with her mother. She was severely mentally handicapped and loved music. Mary Beth knew the sister would have no idea what was going on, or what she should do, so she pulled her to the floor and lay on top of her. (The girl had wanted to get up to see what was happening.) Mary Beth was subsequently shot in the back. Yet she refused to get up even though she was bleeding. That day she very likely saved her friend's sister's life. Mary Beth recovered from her wound, completed her college degree, and is now a school teacher.

By this we know love, because He laid down His life for us. And we also ought to lay down our lives for the brethren.
—1 John 3:16

Do you recall the quality listed as the very first fruit of the Spirit? *"But the fruit of the Spirit is love, joy, peace, longsuffering, kindness, goodness, faithfulness, gentleness, self-control. Against such there is no law"* (Galatians 5:22–23). If you truly have Christ abiding in you and you in Him—the Holy Spirit resident in you—then your life will be characterized first of all by love.

In other words, the way people will know that we belong to Christ is if our actions, our attitudes, our behavior, our strategy, and our focus in life revolve around love—and joy, peace, longsuffering, kindness, goodness, faithfulness, gentleness, and self-control.

The Greatest of These Is Love

In the "love chapter," 1 Corinthians 13, Paul eloquently describes the incredible importance of love. He says, *"I may be able to speak the languages of human beings and even of angels, but if I have no love, my speech is no more than a noisy gong or a clanging bell. I may have the gift of inspired preaching; I may have all knowledge and understand all secrets; I may have all the faith needed to move mountains—but if I have no love, I am nothing. I may give away everything I have, and even give up my body to be burned—but if I have no love, this does me no good"* (1 Corinthians 13:1–3 GNT).

In perhaps the most compelling treatise on love ever written, Paul recognizes that there are a lot of things that can act as motivations in our life. But when everything is said and done, when all that life has to offer is boiled down into the pure essence of what God intended, when all the fluff and accoutrements of life are burned away, only three pure things remain. Paul asserts, *"Right now three things remain: faith, hope, and love. But the greatest of these is love"* (1 Corinthians 13:13 ISV).

Hope is what keeps people going through the difficult times.

Faith gives people direction in their life. Hebrews 11:1 describes faith as a *"confidence"* of things hoped for (YLT). Other translators use the words *assurance* (ISV) or *substance* (NKJV). Faith is what we base our lives upon. It gives us focus, motivation, and even our identity as people. It is the truth upon which we base our life; the confidence we have in God that He is who He says He is and that He will do what He says He will do. *"Now without faith it is impossible to please God, for whoever comes to him must believe that he exists and that he rewards those who diligently search for him"* (Hebrews 11:6 ISV).

Hope is what keeps people going through the difficult times. It is what people cling to when nothing else seems to be making sense. Without hope, people give up and despair. Hope gives people confidence that the future will be well worth the present sacrifices we must make. Paul describes hope as *"an anchor of the soul, both sure and steadfast"* (Hebrews 6:9). The Word tells us that we hope

- to share in God's glory (Romans 5:2);

- in the resurrection of the righteous (Acts 24:15);

- for our adoption, the redemption of our bodies (Romans 8:23-24);

- to know the riches of His glorious inheritance among the saints (Ephesians 1:18);

- that we will have nothing to be ashamed of when Christ returns (Philippians 1:20);

- to experience the resurrection of the dead (Philippians 3:11);

- in Christ Jesus our Lord (1 Timothy 1:1);

- in the living God (1 Timothy 4:10); and

- in eternal life which God has promised before the world began (Titus 1:2).

But nevertheless, faith and hope do not compare to the surpassing quality and nature of love. As Christ Himself said, all of the Law and the Prophets can be summed up in two commands: *"Love the Lord your God"* and *"love your neighbor"* (Matthew 22:37–40).

■ ■ ■

Would the church survive the vote
and even continue to exist?

■ ■ ■

Chapter 4

Love Gone Wrong

It had been seven years since Keystone Community Church's first official Sunday service. Many people had come through the doors, various staff had been employed, and many dreams had been realized in the planting of a young congregation in this growing neighborhood. But today the members were voting on whether or not to fire their founding pastor. He had not been involved in immoral activity, questionable behavior, or personal burnout or failure. In fact, he was the reason most of the people were at the church in the first place! But the board felt the church needed to move in a new direction and that they needed a new pastor to take them there.

There was no question that many of the families who loved and supported the pastor would leave if he were fired, but many others would leave if he remained. How did they get to this point? Would the church survive the vote and even continue to exist? It seemed too late to take a step back seeking the Lord together as a congregation, praying for reconciliation. Several members wondered what the people in their community would think; others wondered exactly what Christ thought about what was happening to this church— His body.

Most churches begin with the best of intentions. Some are birthed as intentional church plants; others start as reactions to or divisions of other established churches. Some develop out of a flourishing Bible study group; others are the result of revival that has broken out in a particular region. Often those who start a church desire that it look like the early churches described in the New Testament Book of Acts and in Paul's letters. There are those who believe the New Testament model is to meet in people's homes and cite Rome (Romans 16:5), Corinth (1 Corinthians 16:19), and Colosse (Colossians 4:15) as examples. Others point to the many thousands God added to the church in Jerusalem (Acts 4:4) as what God intended as a model for a church. Regardless of size, focus, location, or design, nearly every church begins with the heart desire of reaching people for God, caring for its members, and making a positive difference in its community.

A Closer Look at Ephesus

Certainly the New Testament offers insights into what the first churches looked like at their best, but it also describes what can happen to churches if they are not vigilant to adhere to their core values and God-given priorities. Both the Apostles Paul and John draw attention to how Christ's churches can go off track and travel down roads that lead them far away from where they imagined they would end up. Churches are easily enticed to chase after distractions and focus on secondary priorities. In some cases, they can even lose touch with Christ altogether Who, after all, is the head of His church. The church in Ephesus is a good example of how a congregation can stray from its primary purposes of loving God and loving its neighbors.

The church in the city of Ephesus, known at its height as the first and greatest metropolis of Asia, had a great start. In fact, they had some of the strongest founders of any of the first churches. It was here that the Apostle Paul helped to establish a young congregation of believers in the Way, the movement of Jesus followers that had formed after the advent of Pentecost in Jerusalem. On Paul's return from his second missionary journey to Jerusalem, he visited Ephesus for a few months and left Aquila and Priscilla behind to carry on the work of spreading the gospel. He returned again on his third missionary journey and stayed for some three years, where the impact of his ministry reportedly reached far and wide throughout Asia Minor.

Listen to how Paul describes the believers in his letter to those residing in this important and influential city.

> *To God's people in Ephesus, who are faithful in their life in union with Christ Jesus...For this reason, ever since I heard of your faith in the Lord Jesus and your love for all God's people, I have not stopped giving thanks to God for you. I remember you in my prayers and ask the God of our Lord Jesus Christ, the glorious Father, to give you the Spirit, who will make you wise and reveal God to you, so that you will know him...I ask God from the wealth of his glory to give you power through his Spirit to be strong in your inner selves, and I pray that Christ will make his home in your hearts through faith. I pray that you may have your roots and foundation in love, so that you, together with all God's people, may have the power to understand how broad and long, how high and deep, is Christ's love. Yes, may you come to know his love— although it can never be fully known—and so be completely filled with the very nature of God...Since you are God's dear children, you must try to be like him. Your life must be controlled by love, just as Christ loved us and gave his life for us as a sweet-smelling offering and sacrifice that pleases God...May God's grace be with all those who love our Lord Jesus Christ with undying love.*
> —Ephesians 1:1, 15–17; 3:16–19; 5:1–2; 6:24 (GNT)

Clearly Paul had great affection and fond memories toward the members of the church in Ephesus. He had intimate knowledge of their lives as anyone would who had lived and worked among them for so long. Ephesus was also the home base for a strong ministry couple named Priscilla and Aquila who discipled these new believers. The evangelist Apollos also did much to expand the kingdom of God there and elsewhere. Luke the evangelist also sheds light on Paul's relationship to the Ephesians in his record of the Acts of the Apostles as he describes Paul's last visit to his dear friends there. Here we see their mutual affection and deep emotions expressed for one another as Paul prepares to leave for Jerusalem where he would ultimately be arrested.

From Miletus he sent to Ephesus and called for the elders of the church. And when they had come to him, he said to them: "You know, from the first day that I came to Asia, in what manner I always lived among you, serving the Lord with all humility, with many tears and trials which happened to me by the plotting of the Jews; how I kept back nothing that was helpful, but proclaimed it to you, and taught you publicly and from house to house, testifying to Jews, and also to Greeks, repentance toward God and faith toward our Lord Jesus Christ. And see, now I go bound in the spirit to Jerusalem, not knowing the things that will happen to me there, except that the Holy Spirit testifies in every city, saying that chains and tribulations await me...For I know this, that after my departure savage wolves will come in among you, not sparing the flock. Also from among yourselves men will rise up, speaking perverse things, to draw away the disciples after themselves. Therefore watch, and remember that for three years I did not cease to warn everyone night and day with tears."...And when he had said these things, he knelt down and prayed with them all. Then they all wept freely, and fell on Paul's neck and kissed him, sorrowing most of all for the words which he spoke,

that they would see his face no more. And they accompa-
nied him to the ship.
—Acts 20:17–23, 29–31, 36–38

The historical record shows the church in Ephesus to be healthy, growing, and exemplary in their love for God and for those who ministered among them. Paul, Aquila and Priscilla, and Apollos had modeled for them how to live as believers and how to honor Christ in their interaction with one another and behavior toward outsiders. Paul even sent his young protégé Timothy to disciple them in doctrine and practice (1 Timothy 1:3). And evidently the church was sufficiently strong and developed enough to grow and train up their own young men in the Lord, two of whom became important companions to Paul in his travels and minis-try. Trophimus and Tychicus were helpful to Paul, and Tychicus was sent numerous times as an encourager to various churches on his behalf. Later, the Apostle John is also said to have lived in Ephesus, perhaps taking care of Jesus' mother, Mary, there. Other churches may have envied Ephesus for being blessed enough to have Paul and John and the others live in their city and work in their church for as long as they did. This was a church where any modern Christian would have been wholeheartedly welcomed, carefully discipled, and dearly loved. No wonder it was considered an important church among the seven churches in what is today western Turkey.

Love Lost

However, something changed in Ephesus—a change that was potentially devastating and disastrous. During a time of inten-sifying persecution and John's subsequent exile to the island of Patmos, the people's hearts began to shift. Perhaps they became distracted by the constant threats from antagonists outside the church. Paul also had warned them about wolves who were trying to come in to harm the flock as well as corrupt mem-bers from within who were intent on dividing and destroying the fellowship (Acts 20:29–30). Maybe they had not heeded Paul's warnings and instead allowed forceful people to introduce errant doctrines in their midst. Perhaps they were distracted by various ministry projects to those who were needy among them. Maybe they became overly involved in local politics, various community affairs, or social issues. One wonders if they had become overly weary of outsiders or too suspicious of one another for fear of false doctrines infiltrating their camp. Who can say? Whatever the cause, the result was a change in heart among the membership and a loss of love for God and for one another.

How do we know? We know because Christ Himself sends a very strong and accusatory message through the Apostle John directly to the church in Ephesus. This is recorded in the final book of the Bible, Revelation, chapters 1–3. Here Jesus gives His assessment of the seven churches in Asia Minor, including Ephesus. Although the Ephesian believers displayed some very noble and commendable aspects of character, the Lord they claimed to serve gave them a failing grade.

> *"To the angel of the church of Ephesus write, 'These things says He who holds the seven stars in His right hand, who walks in the midst of the seven golden lampstands: "I know your works, your labor, your patience, and that you cannot bear those who are evil. And you have tested those who say they are apostles and are not, and have found them liars; and you have persevered and have patience, and have labored for My name's sake and have not become weary. Nevertheless I have this against you, that you have left your first love. Remember therefore from where you have fallen; repent and do the first works, or else I will come to you quickly and remove your lampstand from its place—unless you repent."'"*
> —Revelation 2:1–5

If the Ephesian church were a modern-day church we likely would have given it great accolades rather than a harsh rebuke.

We might even have presented it with an "Outstanding Church of the Year" award. First, they were working hard for God's kingdom, and they were well known for their patience, a rare and much sought-after quality. Second, they exhibited spiritual discernment and were able to quickly identify evildoers in their midst and exclude pretenders in the faith. Third, they had persevered amid much suffering and great trials, a characteristic that only a faithful few have in abundance. Today, we might hold this church up before others as an example of everything a church should be. But Christ, the Head of His churches, the Lord over His body, looked into their hearts and found something seriously amiss. The very thing Paul had so strongly commended them for in his personal letter to them years earlier was gone—and sadly they had not even noticed its absence.

Have another look at the Ephesians passages. Look at what Paul has to say specifically about their love.

I heard of your faith in the Lord Jesus and your love for all the saints.
—Ephesians 1:15

I pray that you may have your roots and foundation in love, so that you, together with all God's people, may have the power to understand how broad and long, how high and deep, is Christ's love. Yes, may you come to know his love.
—Ephesians 3:17–19 (GNT)

Your life must be controlled by love.
—Ephesians 5:2 (GNT)

May God's grace be with all those who love our Lord Jesus Christ with undying love.
—Ephesians 6:24 (GNT)

How was it that such a strong church, such an active church, such an important church could actually be accused of not having love? Anyone looking at the church probably would never have come to such a conclusion. But it is not our opinion that really matters; it is the opinion of Christ that counts.

According to Christ's assessment, despite all the commendable activity that was evident from outside appearances, what mattered to Him was what was on the inside—the condition of their hearts. They were busy for the kingdom, busy rooting out evil, busy assessing the theological and doctrinal differences of those who came to them, busy standing against persecution, busy being busy.

I like how *Revelation: Four Views: A Parallel Commentary* puts it: "Like Martha, a church may become so engrossed in religious work that it neglects the 'one thing needed' (Luke 10:42). No amount of religious orthodoxy, labor, or loyalty can make up for a deficit in Christian love (1 Cor. 13:2–3)." In the midst of their busyness they had lost their love for God and for one another and as a result, the judgment of God was at hand. They had started strong and well, but they were ending weak and poor. Today, the archaeological evidence of this church is scattered rubble and stone fragments among the ruins of what once was one of the most influential cities of the Roman Empire. The *Four Views* commentary on Revelation puts it this way: "The loss of love is no minor defect, but constitutes a fallen state of the church, requiring that they repent and do the first works."

Let's consider another church mentioned alongside Ephesus in the Book of Revelation. Jesus says to the Laodiceans:

> """*So then, because you are lukewarm, and neither cold nor hot, I will vomit you out of My mouth. Because you say, 'I am rich, have become wealthy, and have need of*

> It is not our opinion that really matters; it is the opinion of Christ that counts.

nothing'—and do not know that you are wretched, miser-
able, poor, blind, and naked—I counsel you to buy from
Me gold refined in the fire, that you may be rich; and
white garments, that you may be clothed, that the shame
of your nakedness may not be revealed; and anoint your
eyes with eye salve, that you may see. As many as I love,
I rebuke and chasten. Therefore be zealous and repent.
Behold, I stand at the door and knock. If anyone hears
My voice and opens the door, I will come in to him and
dine with him, and he with Me. To him who overcomes
I will grant to sit with Me on My throne, as I also over-
came and sat down with My Father on His throne. He
who has an ear, let him hear what the Spirit says to the
churches."'"
—Revelation 3:16–22

When Jesus walked in the midst of this particular church, he heard them commenting on how well they thought they were doing! They all believed they were wealthy, healthy, and in need of nothing! But Christ looked under the surface and found them to be "wretched, miserable, poor, blind, and naked." How different is Christ's assessment from the church's assessment of itself? The difference is like night and day! Exact opposites. They had so deceived themselves that they thought they were doing great when, according to Christ, they had completely lost their useful-ness in His hands and needed to be vomited out.

Notice that Christ ends up standing outside the church door repeatedly knocking and calling for someone to please open the door and let Him back in! Incredible. I want to know how Jesus got on the outside in the first place! What was it that caused the church members to push Him out of the center of their church life, to lock Him out of their activities, to shun Him from their planning, to prohibit His presence in their worship, and to keep Him away from their relationships? They had not only lost touch with the Head of their church, they had expelled Him from their presence and bolted the door. No wonder Christ is about to remove their "candlestick." I don't think they were even a functioning church. They were a community club, a social group, a religious society, a gathering, but not a body of Christ. Oh, that we may anoint our eyes with salve and see what is actually going on in some of our churches. We may think we're doing fine, but what does Christ think?

Upon Closer Examination

Christ looks with a keen and discerning eye at our church's ministries and event calendar; He sees our schedule of activities. He searches through our church constitutions, operating manuals, and policy documents. He is looking for the one thing that He has ordained must be the most basic and fundamental characteristic of His body, the church—and that is love.

When Christ was asked which of all the commandments was the greatest He replied, "'*You shall love the Lord your God with all your heart, with all your soul, and with all your mind.' This is the first and great commandment. And the second is like it: 'You shall love your neighbor as yourself'*" (Matthew 22:37–39). I hope you noticed that this verse does not say we are to "serve" God with all of our heart, or to make "sacrifices" to God or "minister in His name" with all of our heart. Why? Because if our service, sacrifice, or ministry does not emanate from love, they are not in any way pleasing to God. Regardless of what anyone says, I can assure you that if Christ were asked to select the greatest commandments today, His answer would still be the same!

We may think we're doing fine, but what does Christ think?

Some church ministries, calendars, and programs are so extensive they make major university class schedules look like child's play. Yet when a newcomer walks through the door on Sunday, while they may be inundated with requests to sign up for activities or put their children in programs, there is little evidence of Christ's number one priority among the members. They are told to "come to this event," "support this activity," "give to that project," "pray for this family," "bring food for this cause," and they see people who are so incredibly busy that they may not even notice that they have lost their first love.

In so many churches, it appears people have jettisoned loving one another and replaced it with good deeds or keeping busy or working hard. There are Bible studies, children's ministries, women's events, men's retreats, youth outreach activities, and on and on—a veritable cornucopia of things in which to get involved. But these activities are not necessarily evidence of genuine love.

Let me give a shocking example from my own experience of a church that lost its love. This body in which I served as an associate had become so divided that the church leaders (representing several key families) were pitted against the senior pastor. On several occasions, these men had met together and voted among themselves to ask the pastor to resign. On one particular evening, I received a phone call from the pastor asking that I pray for him as the deacons were having a meeting next door at the church, and he expected them to visit his home asking for his resignation yet again. And once again, he planned on refusing to resign. Whenever the pastor was preaching, these leaders would sit on the back pew with their arms folded across their chests, wagging their disapproving heads at him. As months passed, the tension became so severe between those who supported the pastor and those who sought his resignation that I doubt any acceptable worship took place in that church. The rift came to a head one Sunday morning when the pastor had a stroke and passed out on the platform. As a young part-time minister, I was confounded and shocked at what was taking place in front of my eyes. Power struggles of all kinds, with roots both in the pew and in the pulpit, wreak havoc in many churches today, and bring spiritual devastation upon the members for generations, particularly among the young or those new in faith.

For his book, *Parenting Prodigals: Six Principles for Bringing Your Son or Daughter Back to God,* Phil Waldrep interviewed hundreds of men and women who abandoned the church or Christianity altogether (some of whom have returned; some not). Many of his interviewees were the children of pastors. In a surprisingly high number of cases, the catalyst for turning their backs on church and God's people was a church fight or a church split. The incredible damage that has been done to young Christians over the years by unloving and uncaring people within the church is nearly unforgivable. How many children and young people have witnessed screaming matches during business meetings, or seen their fathers fired by hot-headed church leaders, or listened to the ranting of out-of-control deacons against their pastor. It's hardly a wonder they have decided never again to darken the doors of a church. Many a young Christian's faith has been shipwrecked due to unthinking, ungodly, unloving people in the church—whether they be pastors, deacons, lay leaders, or others—who have vented their frustrations and rage at their brothers or sisters in Christ rather than lovingly confronting them with humility and grace.

I have served as a minister of education in several churches. One Sunday a woman marched up to me, looked over her glasses, and demanded her Sunday School teacher's book, which had not yet arrived in the mail. I tried to explain that it was delayed at customs crossing the border, but we were expecting it to come any day, but she snapped at me and said, "If you were in the secular world, you would have been fired a long time ago!" She spun on her heels and walked away. I felt like she had just vomited on me, and I had to clean up the mess. Fortunately I know that pastors are often lightning rods that attract the fallout from people's bad weeks. We are a pretty safe target, because we know it is not in our own best interest to fight back! I learned that this woman was anxious and afraid due to a potentially life-threatening medical diagnosis given to her a few days earlier. But her contemptuous behavior at church did nothing to garner sympathy from others.

Paul wanted the church to exude an aroma of love, to have the fragrance of grace, to radiate compassion, and to be known everywhere for their deep and abiding fellowship between brothers and sisters in Christ. To the church in Philippi he writes:

Therefore

- *if there is any consolation in Christ,*
- *if any comfort of love,*
- *if any fellowship of the Spirit,*
- *if any affection and mercy,*

fulfill my joy by

- *being like-minded,*
- *having the same love,*
- *being of one accord,*
- *of one mind.*

Let nothing be done through selfish ambition or conceit, but in lowliness of mind let each esteem others better than himself. Let each of you look out not only for his own interests, but also for the interests of others.
—Philippians 2:1–4

Love Runs Deep

There is a Greek word used in the New Testament that we have translated into English as several words, but most often it is translated as *fellowship*, as in Acts 2:42, *"And they continued steadfastly in the apostles' doctrine and fellowship, in the breaking of bread, and in prayers."* But it also can mean partnership, communion, communication, participation, companionship, and benefaction, according to *Strong's Concordance*. Fellowship, or *koinonia* (pronounced coin-o-NEE-a), is the natural result when church members love one another. It is lost when love is absent.

The kind of fellowship the New Testament church knew was not another word for "potluck dinner" or "coffee time," it was a deep and sacrificial commitment of loyalty toward one another based on the unifying character of the Spirit of God residing in each person. In the first churches, after Communion or the Lord's Supper, there often followed a meal of sorts, a "love feast" or an *agape* (pronounced a-GAH-pay) meal. Little is known about this meal other than the corrective instructions Paul has provided in 1 Corinthians 11:20–34 in reaction to those who were misusing this time together. The "love feast" has generally not survived over the centuries, but for many churches the sharing of food has remained a great way to "fellowship" with one another.

How do you know if *koinonia* is missing from your church? In many ways it is like going through the motions without the meaning. The actions are there but the heart is not. The worship may be lively and people may even clap their hands. The bulletin can be full of activities and programs, and people generally are quite busy. The pastor will smile and shake people's hands at the exit door, and the parking lot is often mostly full. But the auditorium will empty quickly after the service, very few people will loiter in the foyer, there will be an absence of laughter, little to no hugging, and every family will go directly home or out to lunch alone. Visitors rarely come back twice, there are lots of little fires to put out during the week, people get their feelings hurt easily and are protective of their areas of ministry. The polite social interaction in the foyer rarely if ever gets past the surface, and people do not feel connected to one another. The pastor wonders what is really going on in the hearts and minds of his congregation, and the congregation wonders if anyone really cares what is going on in their lives. They are often reluctant to share prayer requests because it seems the prayer list is more for information or gossip than a means of lifting one another up before the throne of grace. What breaks my heart is to know for a fact that this is what many people feel is "normal" for church. It is not. It may be normal for some churches, but it is a far cry from what Christ expects from His people.

Koinonia is more than fellowship. It is more than working together. It is more than accomplishing goals and projects together. It is a deep and abiding love for one another that includes an unreserved and immediate willingness to sacrifice for one another. *"But if we walk in the light as He is in the light, we have fellowship* [koinonia] *with one another, and the blood of Jesus Christ His Son cleanses us from all sin"* (1 John 1:7). Walking in the light represents being filled with God's Spirit; when He is living in us, we will then be able to truly fellowship with other Christians.

When all else fails, love won't.

Koinonia was essential to the survival of the early church. It was the glue that held the church together. It was love in action, and the bond that helped church members survive in the midst of tremendous persecution. Peter's letters were written at one of the most challenging times faced by the early church. He knew that without love, the church could not withstand the attacks of the Jews on one side and the Romans on the other. He writes, *"Above all, continue to love each other deeply, because love covers a multitude of sins. Show hospitality to one another without complaining. As good servant managers of God's grace in its various forms, serve one another with the gift each of you has received"* (1 Peter 4:8–10 ISV). When all else fails, love won't.

Three Critical Commands

To put it simply: love.

> *And whatever we ask we receive from Him, because we keep His commandments and do those things that are pleasing in His sight. And this is His commandment: that we should believe on the name of His Son Jesus Christ and love one another, as He gave us commandment. Now he who keeps His commandments abides in Him, and He in him. And by this we know that He abides in us, by the Spirit whom He has given us.*
> —1 John 3:22–24

This is a very important passage of Scripture. It is significant that John mentions just two commands of God—believe in His Son, which is paramount, and love one another. Once we have trusted in God's Son, John apparently is telling us that loving one another is the primary goal. Why, I wonder, did Christ need to command us to love? Would it not be something that naturally occurs among God's people? Would love not just flow from one believer to another because of the indwelling presence of the Spirit of God? Apparently not. It seems that unless Christ mandates this as a priority issue, we will naturally neglect it or abandon it as unnecessary or nonessential. I suppose it shouldn't be a surprise that people have trouble loving others when we see the Apostle Paul instructing husbands to love their wives (Colossians 3:19) and instructing women to love their husbands and their children (Titus 2:4)!

Christ wants love to be ever in the forefront of our minds and hearts. Above all other attributes Christ wants His followers to be known by their love. If we truly believe in Him as God commanded, then we will truly love one another as Christ commanded.

John goes on to say that if we obey God's commands, we live in union with Him. Our obedience brings us in line with God's heart, and He is then able to use us as His instruments of righteousness. Our obedience thus determines our usefulness in His hands. The activity of God's Spirit in and through us is the evidence that we are living in accordance with Christ's commands. When we do not sense the presence of God's Spirit in our life, or when there is a lack of God's power or authority in our ministry, we can be confident there is an obedience problem in our life.

Never stop praying.

> *Pray without ceasing.*
> —1 Thessalonians 5:17

> *Continue earnestly in prayer, being vigilant in it with thanksgiving.*
> —Colossians 4:2

> *Pray on every occasion, as the Spirit leads. For this reason keep alert and never give up; pray always for all God's people.*
> —Ephesians 6:18

> *Then those who gladly received his word were baptized; and that day about three thousand souls were added to them. And they continued steadfastly in the apostles' doctrine and fellowship, in the breaking of bread, and in prayers.*
> —Acts 2:41–42

What does prayer have to do with love? Prayer reflects the desire of God's people to draw close to His heart. So, a person's prayer life is a measure of the depth of a person's love for God. The fact of the matter is that people want to spend time with those they love. Believers spend time with God when they open the Bible and search out a word from their heavenly Father, or when they offer praises and songs of worship, or when they kneel in His presence talking with Him and allowing Him to speak back into their life through His Spirit.

When a church offers little time for their members to come together in prayer, or when leaders do not model prayerfulness for their members, there is a heart problem. It is my belief that a prayerless church is a loveless church. The depth of a church's commitment to prayer is a good indicator of the level of love the people have for God and for one another.

- Is there a regularly scheduled prayer time where the body can come together to seek God?

- Are there specially called prayer gatherings during times of decision-making such as hiring staff, building programs, beginning a mission, or seeking a new direction for ministry?

- Is prayer a central part of the worship service?

- Do the pastor(s) and staff model praying for their people on a regular basis?

- Is prayer taught, talked about, promoted, and valued in the congregation?

- Does the church have a prayer ministry that covers the church body and its activities with prayer?

Prayer also provides a great opportunity to get to know your fellow church members on a deeper level. When you hear your brothers and sisters in Christ pouring out their heart to our heavenly Father and bringing one another's needs and concerns to God in prayer, you will grow in your love and appreciation for them. Just as husbands and wives who pray together have stronger marriages, church members who come together to pray with one another will have both a stronger church and a deeper love for one another.

If a congregation is not praying together, there will be a considerable lack in intimacy, fellowship, and regard for one another's interests. The body of Christ is a spiritual body with Christ as the Head. It is as though Christ's Spirit is the blood coursing through the veins of each member, drawing them closer to the Father and to one another as they pray. *"But he who is joined to the Lord is one spirit with Him"* (1 Corinthians 6:17). There is no reason for God's people not to be of one heart and one mind when they pray together, as there is only one Spirit and one Lord. God is not divided, and neither should we be. *"There is one body and one Spirit, just as there is one hope to which God has called you. There is one Lord, one faith, one baptism; there is one God and Father of all, who is Lord of all, works through all, and is in all"* (Ephesians 4:4–6 GNT). God uses prayer to grow us in our love for Him and for one another.

> **The body of Christ is a spiritual body with Christ as the Head.**

Be reconciled.

> *All of this comes from God, who has reconciled us to himself through the Messiah and has given us the ministry of reconciliation.*
> —2 Corinthians 5:18 (ISV)

It is almost inconceivable that God's people would choose to harm one another rather than love one another, but it happens all too often in the church. They refuse to be reconciled with their brother or sister at church, sometimes over very minor issues and misunderstandings. That "root of bitterness" can grow into a full-fledged tree in the lives of believers who choose not to forgive those who have done them wrong. Men and women are deliberately grieving the Holy Spirit, who is at work in their lives, if they continue to live at odds with fellow members and to hold grudges against them.

Ken Sande wrote a wonderful book with Tom Raabe called *Peacemaking for Families: A Biblical Guide to Managing Conflict in Your Home.* Although this book aims to help families bring resolution to conflict, the principles apply equally well to the church family—brothers and sisters in Christ. Anytime more than one person is present in a room there is potential for conflict. However, love for one another can bring quick resolution both in a family and in the church. But when love is absent, conflict can grow into an out-of-control monster that wreaks havoc in the body of Christ, destroying one church after another. *"Above all, continue to love each other deeply, because love covers a multitude of sins"* (1 Peter 4:8 ISV). Where love is present, there is safety in the midst of conflict and forgiveness readily at hand. When love is present, peacemakers are able to perform their craft with effective ease. As Christ said, *"Blessed are the peacemakers, for they shall be called sons of God"* (Matthew 5:9).

Love for one another can bring quick resolution both in a family and in the church.

The need to be reconciled with a fellow church member is more important to God than your worship. *"'So if you are presenting your gift at the altar and remember there that your brother has something against you, leave your gift there before the altar and first go and be reconciled to your brother. Then come and offer your gift'"* (Matthew 5:23–24 ISV). Many people who think they are worshipping God on Sunday are actually only performing unacceptable and empty religious activities since they have chosen to let their desire for revenge or self-pity overrule Jesus' command to love. For those who refuse to be reconciled to their brother or sister in Christ, who insist on holding grudges and acting in unloving ways toward others in the church, their very relationship with God is in serious need of repair. Be reconciled to your brother or sister and be reconciled to God. Don't put off an opportunity to show love if it is in your power to do so.

■ ■ ■

Many people were drawn to this church,
because it asked little of those who attended
and was designed to make outsiders feel comfortable.

■ ■ ■

Chapter 5

Love Denied

A well-established church hired a new lead pastor with the mandate to develop a strategy to guide it into the twenty-first century. He arrived with a stack of church growth books and a prepackaged plan to renovate the church's character, focus, drive, and direction, which pleased the board members very much. His goal was to make the church's worship service contemporary and cutting-edge, establish satellite congregations around the city, implement a staff-driven model to streamline ministries, and become the place where the community would turn in times of need. Over the next four years, a new auditorium and office suite were built, leaders were hired to renovate the worship services, the sermons included multimedia, the men left their ties at home, and a coffee bar was installed in the foyer. Many people were drawn to this church, because it asked little of those who attended and was designed to make outsiders feel comfortable. But as the ship drastically changed course, some of its passengers became unsettled at the breakneck speed of change and opted to jump ship rather than continue in a direction they had not signed on for. A full 30 to 40 percent of the membership left the church frustrated, disillusioned, and hurt spiritually and emotionally. The pastor told the leadership board that he no longer had time for visionless people and that it was their responsibility to deal with disgruntled members. So people kept leaving.

Family after family found other churches where they felt safe and cared for. The church they had joined before this new pastor arrived seemed no longer to exist. What was even more heartbreaking was that the members who remained began to feel abandoned by their friends. They became resentful either towards the departing members or the staff who refused to go after them and try to bring them back. Those who left were hurt and disillusioned and those who remained were hurt and frustrated. Most just thought this was the price of progress. Sadly many of the leaders stood by silently as all this unfolded, instead of stepping in to try to halt the damage being done. Critics of the regime were routinely dismissed as disloyal or having critical spirits. Their concerns over the destruction of the body were never taken seriously.

This kind of scenario is not always entirely the fault of an often well-meaning pastor either. Church boards and leadership groups often look to the corporate business model to give their church direction, and want a CEO to administrate their programs rather than a shepherd to guide the sheep. Churches need shepherds who will love all of God's people rather than leave the weak and slow in the dust as they press on into a "cutting-edge" future. If Christians are to be known for our love, we cannot sacrifice our people to accomplish grand vision statements and church growth goals. Struggling, hurting, and neglected people cannot be viewed as hindrances to a goal; rather, taking our cue from Jesus, they should be our priority.

Vision statements have become very popular in churches. These slogans become a part of the church identity. They are not only emblazoned on walls and bulletins, but on the minds and in the hearts of the people. Some of these slogans change every year as the staff and leaders redirect their church's ministry.

Others reflect the heart of the pastor and remain in place as long as he is leading the church. Slogans can be good when they remind people of what is important and when they help keep the main thing the main thing.

Struggling, hurting, and neglected people cannot be viewed as hindrances.

The slogan I used throughout my tenure as a senior pastor was taken in part from Paul's letter to the believers in Colosse: "Encouraged in Heart, United in Love, Equipped for Impact." It should be no surprise that the focus of my preaching, the character of our congregation, the emphasis in our various ministries, and the way in which we conducted ourselves in the community all reflected this emphasis. As I read Paul's encouraging letter to this new church, I identify with his heart for his brothers and sisters in Christ. And that's my heart as I write this chapter.

> *For I want you to know how much I struggle for you, for those in Laodicea, and for all who have never seen me face to face. Because they are united in love, I pray that their hearts may be encouraged by all the riches that come from a complete understanding of the full knowledge of the Messiah, who is the mystery of God. In him are hidden all the treasures of wisdom and knowledge. I say this so that no one will mislead you with nice-sounding rhetoric. For although I am physically absent, I am with you in spirit, rejoicing to see how stable you are and how firm your faith in the Messiah is. So then, just as you have received the Messiah Jesus the Lord, continue to live dependent on him. For you have been rooted in him and are being built up and strengthened in the faith, just as you were taught, while you continue to be thankful.*
> —Colossians 2:1–7 (ISV)

As we struggle together, I want to examine the stumbling blocks that hinder the expression of Christ-like love in the church. How do God's people, who should be characterized by His love, cease to demonstrate love to one another? I want to answer this question so that we can begin a journey to bring back love in the church.

Weak Foundations

Paul sought to encourage believers to build on the strong foundation of knowing Christ, because when you know Him, you know His heart, His passion, and His will for your life. Once you are "rooted" in Him and "are being built up and strengthened in the faith," you will not be susceptible to false teachings or get off track in your priorities or the focus of your ministries. If you've ever dug up a tree stump, then you've discovered just how extensive the support system is under a tree. Unless you have some massive hydraulic equipment, the roots of a tree are not easily removed.

If you've ever built a building from the ground up, you also know the tremendous importance of the foundation, the part no one ever sees after the building is completed. The foundation must be able to bear what is going to be placed on top of it and sturdy enough to withstand the forces of nature. Even when the building is blown away in a hurricane or tornado, almost without exception, the foundation will remain. The safety of the structure depends on how well it is fixed to the foundation. Paul says here that he rejoices *"to see how stable you are and how firm your faith in the Messiah is"* (Colossians 2:5 ISV). It is not difficult to conclude that the closer we are to Christ, the more we will look like the church He expects us to be. The farther away we get from our relationship with Christ, the less we will look like Him and reflect His heart and love for others.

Jesus said, *"'I am the vine, you are the branches. He who abides in Me, and I in him, bears much fruit; for without Me you can do nothing. If anyone does not abide in Me, he is cast out as a branch and is withered; and they gather them and throw them into the fire, and they are burned'"* (John 15:5–6). If we are not abiding in Christ it will be impossible for us to demonstrate His heart for others.

This particular chapter is very difficult for me to write. It grieves me to know the trauma that goes on in the name of "religion," "service to God," and "ministry." Many actions in the church are motivated by anger, lust, pride, hate, or jealousy rather than by love. As a result, the effectiveness of God's church around the world has been compromised.

In most cases, people are not intentionally trying to hurt others. Instead they justify their actions as being in the best interests of the church. Nevertheless, if they are motivated by anything other than love, the effect likely will be to tear apart the body rather than build it up. It is discouraging to watch the body of Christ—those who are His hands and feet, the ones who hold the message of love in their hands and in their hearts—wander so far away from a foundational relationship with Christ. They are actually demonstrating the character qualities that are exactly the opposite of those of the One they claim to serve! Inevitably, when God's people let their guard down and wander away from their first love, these things—anger, lust, pride, hatred—multiply.

> The farther away we get from our relationship with Christ, the less we will look like Him.

When we neglect our relationship with God, we fall back into our old ways—factions, hatred, slander, criticism, arrogance, selfish ambition, racism, bigotry, manipulation, coercion, abuse of power, politicking, and influence peddling. Spending time with God keeps us centered on His agenda rather than our own and focuses our hearts on what is important to Him rather than what may be important to us at the time. It is vital for God's people, particularly those in any kind of leadership, to stay close to Christ, so that they are able to put aside their own personal ambitions and desires and have their minds and hearts truly seeking the will of God for His church. How can the finance committee or outreach committee or missions committee make wise decisions without seeking Christ? How can a pastoral search committee select the right person without asking, "What kind of pastor does God want the church to have?"

"For I know the purposes which I am planning for you," says Jehovah, "purposes of peace, and not for evil; to give you posterity and a hope. Then you shall call on Me, and you shall go and pray to Me, and I will listen to you. And you shall seek and find Me when you search for Me with all your heart."
—Jeremiah 29:11–13 (LITV)

Do you see what God is saying here? He has plans for His people. He has plans for His church. He knows the future and He knows which direction and which focus churches should have to accomplish all He has in mind to do through them. We assume that because we are Christians we already know what His plans are, or that we are able to come up with them on our own. In this passage, the only way we are able to discern God's plans for us and our church is if we are willing to:

■ Call on Him.

■ Come and pray to Him.

■ Seek after Him.

■ Search for Him with all of our heart.

Most of us are quick to call on God in times of need. Many people are faithful to spend time in prayer to God, but fewer really know how to seek after God, and fewer still have the desire to search for God with all of their heart.

God desires that we search for Him with all of our heart, but are we willing to do that? Do we even understand the command to love God with all our heart, all our soul, all our strength, and all our mind? Too often, we are content to let the pastor or other church leaders do the searching and then tell us what to do. When we neglect to seek and search for God, we compromise our ability to serve Him as well. How can we know if what we are doing in the name of

Prayerless churches are loveless churches.

God is actually what He wants us to do? Did we ever actually ask Him?

No Prayer, No Love

When people no longer seek the heart of God through prayer, they cease to reflect His heart of love to others. Prayerless churches are loveless churches. They may be busy churches, good-neighbor churches, active-in-the-community churches, but the love of God will not be manifestly evident in their midst. Few things can create a deeper and more connected intimacy among church members than praying together. When we pray, the Spirit of God, who indwells every true believer, unites our hearts and minds in God.

- When we pray together, we can serve knowing His power and wisdom are working through us.

- When we pray together, we can truly minister in His name, because His Spirit is leading and guiding us.

- When we pray together, we function as His body, bringing hope to a hopeless world and love to desperate people.

- Prayer draws people together with Christ as their center.

- Praying breaks down barriers and draws people to repent and reconcile with one another.

- Prayer opens our heart to what is on the heart of God.

- Prayer prevents God's people from making mistakes, getting off track, and going down the wrong roads.

- Prayer enables us to love those we normally would not be able to love.

One time when we started attending a new church, I was pleased to find out they had an early morning men's prayer time. I set my alarm, laid out my clothes for the next day, and got to bed a bit earlier than usual. When I arrived at the church building, coffee in hand, the parking lot was curiously empty! Two minutes before the prayer time was to start, a small car careened into the parking lot and two associate pastors jumped out. The church doors were quickly unlocked and lights were turned on. I slipped out of my car, locked the door, and entered the building. Where was the pastor? Where were the board members and deacons? Where were the ministry leaders and committee chairmen? We had an opportunity to gather as the body of Christ to seek the heart and mind of God, but almost no one was there. The three of us met at the front of the large auditorium for a few minutes of prayer. We had no prayer list to cover, no Scripture reading with which to prepare our hearts, no sharing of prayer requests—just a quick prayer, and we were on our way. I honestly felt cheated!

I have to tell you I did not sense the power and presence of God that day. Rather, I had a sense we were praying out of duty and obligation, like the brave and the few who must soldier on though everyone else had abandoned us. Two staff members and a visitor were the only people out of 400 members who cared to come before the throne of grace to pray together. It is no wonder to me that I sensed little evidence of God's love or the activity and presence and power of the Holy Spirit in that congregation.

Never underestimate the power of prayer in your church. If you are not actively praying, individually and with others, I believe you will not be fully experiencing the power of God in your life. You will not be seeing the activity of God in your situations and circumstances as you should. You likely will be living day to day without any sense that God is up to something or that He is ready and willing to use you at any time and any place to love others around you. Further, you will feel disconnected to your brothers and sisters in Christ because there is nothing of spiritual significance that is drawing you together. I can also predict that if you have a prayerless church, though your pastor's messages may be well-crafted or entertaining, people's lives will not be transformed by the power of God nor will they be set free from bondage to sin. Broken marriages will not be healed and the scars people carry in their lives will remain. Supernatural love will not characterize your membership.

My father, Henry Blackaby, believes you can tell a lot about a person's spiritual life by the prayers they pray. Your prayers reveal how well you know the One you are talking to. Eloquence and King James language are no substitute for a child of God who knows his Father, hears his Father's voice, and believes He will do as He says He will do. I remember as a young associate pastor attending early morning prayer times at the church and wishing I could just sleep in. We rarely requested anything of God that required God to demonstrate His power. I eventually asked the pastor, "Can we begin to offer prayers that require an act of God to be accomplished? That way we will always know that God has actually intervened in our situations and that a miracle has taken place." That day, the pastor realized we had been expecting very little of a mighty God. To pray prayers worthy of the God we served required us to pray in faith and ask things that only God could do. Prayer should bring the power of God, the presence of God, and the activity of God among His people. When this happens, the love of God will be evident on our faces and in our lives.

Are You Walking in the Spirit or Grieving the Spirit?

Walking in the Spirit is allowing the Holy Spirit to guide our thinking and our actions. On several occasions Paul admonishes us to keep "in step" with the Spirit, to "live" in the Spirit, or to "walk" in the Spirit.

> *I say, then: Walk in the Spirit, and you shall not fulfill the lusts of the flesh.*—Galatians 5:16

> *But if you are led by the Spirit, you are not under the law.*—Galatians 5:18

> *If we live in the Spirit, let us also walk in the Spirit.*
> —Galatians 5:25

Walking in the Spirit, being led by the Spirit, and living in the Spirit shield us from fulfilling the lusts of the flesh and allow us to exhibit the fruit of the Spirit.

> *Now the works of the flesh are evident, which are: adultery, fornication, uncleanness, lewdness, idolatry, sorcery, hatred, contentions, jealousies, outbursts of wrath, selfish ambitions, dissensions, heresies, envy, murders, drunkenness, revelries, and the like; of which I tell you beforehand, just as I also told you in time past, that those who practice such things will not inherit the kingdom of God.*
> —Galatians 5:19–21

This is what it looks like when we avoid the promptings of the Holy Spirit: we demonstrate all the characteristics, values, and morals that are exactly the opposite of love. The impetus, in part, for writing this book was seeing so many of these sinful traits in churches over the years. What this tells me is that too many people are grieving the Holy Spirit personally and corporately.

Experiencing God's Love in the Church

It seems to me that if we are walking in the Spirit, being led by the Spirit, and being filled with the Spirit, then we will see in our lives and churches the character, nature, values, and morals inherent in God's love. What wonders would take place if, at every church business meeting, members demonstrated love, joy, peace, patience, kindness, goodness, faithfulness, gentleness, and self-control! I recall on several occasions sharing a word of caution in a meeting at the right time—thereby de-escalating an increasingly heated discussion—so that the fruit of the Spirit would control us rather than allow the flesh to take control.

> Did you notice the mom coming in late with her two kids in tow without a husband by her side?

Grieving means to ignore God's promptings deliberately, to disregard His commands, and to turn your head away when God puts opportunities for ministry right in front of you. It means refusing to allow God to move you or redirect you from your agenda regardless of what is on His heart.

"And do not grieve the Holy Spirit of God, by whom you were sealed for the day of redemption. Let all bitterness, wrath, anger, clamor, and evil speaking be put away from you, with all malice. And be kind to one another, tenderhearted, forgiving one another, even as God in Christ forgave you" (Ephesians 4:30–32). In 1 Thessalonians 5:19, Paul puts it this way, *"Do not quench the Spirit."*

Did you see the gentleman at church last week sitting alone halfway down the aisle of the auditorium? Did you notice the mom coming in late with her two kids in tow without a husband by her side? Were you aware of the woman who looked distracted, worried, and preoccupied over on the left side? What about the unruly children who were reprimanded by the usher? Did you see the two foreign students who are learning your language and have no one to watch out for them? Were you aware of the young couple who just miscarried their first baby? If you didn't notice those people, you may have grieved the Holy Spirit, ignoring His prompting and invitation to join Him in what He wanted to do to bring a word of encouragement or hope to them. Of course, you can only understand what these people are going through if you first take the time to find out who they are and what their life circumstances are. This is what love looks like in the church. Obeying the Spirit's promptings to risk making a difference in people's lives.

The Spirit does not just help us to be nice people. He leads us to action, to intervene in the eternal destinies of people. There are promptings of the Spirit, little nudges He gives His people to help us notice others and that invite us to become involved in their life or situation. When Philip spotted the Ethiopian reading the Scriptures, the Spirit alerted him to bring illumination to this man's spiritual darkness.

Let's revisit this encounter: *"Now an angel of the Lord spoke to Philip, saying, 'Arise and go toward the south along the road which goes down from Jerusalem to Gaza.' This is desert. So he arose and went. And behold, a man of Ethiopia, a eunuch of great authority under Candace the queen of the Ethiopians, who had charge of all her treasury, and had come to Jerusalem to worship, was returning. And sitting in his chariot, he was reading Isaiah the prophet. Then the Spirit said to Philip, 'Go near and overtake this chariot'"* (Acts 8:26–29).

It is clear the Spirit did not want Philip simply to be a person of outstanding moral character or godly values. He wasn't just supposed to impress the Ethiopian with how nice he was. The Spirit wanted Philip to get up and go over to this government ruler and explain the Scriptures to him. Whether it was a nudge, an impression, a compelling urge, or an out-loud voice, Philip knew without question what God was asking him to do and, fortunately for the official, he obeyed. The Spirit does this all the time. He leads His people to touch other people's lives, to share the gospel message, to explain the Scriptures, to come alongside those in need in order to demonstrate God's love to them.

Let me give an example of the importance of following the prompting of the Holy Spirit. Ministry is challenging at the best of times, and when you add living overseas away from family to that, it can at times become overwhelming. At a time when we were serving abroad and my wife was feeling particularly discouraged and lonely, a pastor's wife from another denomination called saying God had laid it on her heart to invite her to a women's retreat that weekend. She agreed to go and was thoroughly encouraged and renewed in her spirit. It was a timely reminder of God's love for her.

Loving Programs More Than People

If a church is not careful, it will fall into the trap of letting programs, ministries, and events become the primary focus. A church must take care to avoid becoming known for what it *does* as opposed to what it *is*. Even though programs and activities are meant to minister to the body or reach out to the community, they can morph into creatures with relentless appetites that chew people up and spit them out. Some churches begin planning the next annual program as soon as the last one finishes. Hundreds of people are enlisted. At first, they do so willingly. But then after a few years, they have to be cajoled, threatened, made to feel guilty, or shamed into participating. The show must go on, regardless of the many people whose own personal needs go neglected. The show becomes everything and the people are merely there to enable the show/ministry/outreach event to run smoothly and successfully. When the director calls people on the phone, the conversation does not begin with "How are you doing?" or "How can I pray for you?" but "Can you help us out? We really need you this year."

Directors of such events, programs, and ministries, whether volunteers or paid staff, need regular reminders that God does not bless programs; He blesses people. The programs, no matter how wonderful and exciting they are, cannot change people's hearts—only the Spirit of God can do that. The things we do are simply tools God may or may not choose to use to impact the community or the church family. If we ever begin to trust in our programs to reach people rather than trusting in the Spirit of God, He will remove His Spirit and take His hand of blessing from it and leave us to our own devices.

People are always God's priority. Churches that fail to consult with God but mindlessly run the same program year after year after year after monotonous year show that they are trusting in their programs rather than in God. And they wind up paying a heavy price to maintain activities that have long since ceased to be effective. In essence, programs can become gods who rule our lives and sap our time and energy, often with little to show for it in the end. The annual Christmas pageant, outreach event, daily Vacation Bible School, choir tours, mission trips, and summer camps—all can be fun and effective in ministering to people. However, every year someone needs to ask a couple of questions: "Why should we run this program again this year?" and "Is God leading us to do this, or are we only doing it because we did it last year?"

I have watched people run in fear of directors hunting for those they can enlist to help or donate to their programs. Even though the intention may be honorable, the result is that church members do not feel loved, appreciated, or valued when they see the program become the priority instead of the people.

Forgetting That We're Family

Once during a conference question-and-answer time, a man asked me, "What do you do with difficult people in the church?" Immediately my thoughts settled on several possible answers to this question:

1. You can confront them with their divisiveness and suggest they either get on board or find another church—a common approach.

Experiencing God's Love in the Church

2. You can marginalize them or isolate them until they finally get the point and leave.

3. You can call in the "big guns," who can persuade them to settle down and play nice.

4. You can negotiate terms of engagement or reach some sort of compromise so everyone gets something, but no one is really happy in the end.

I followed the example of Jesus and answer the man's question with a question. I replied, "Do you love them?" No one in the audience moved or spoke. I continued, "You see, if you view your fellow members as your enemy, they will act that way. However, if they know without any question that you love them, they will get along with you even when they disagree with some of your decisions." A shepherd may lead the sheep, teach the sheep, disciple the sheep, and visit the sheep, but if he does not love them, he will always have trouble with the flock.

I am capable of reacting strongly at times to those who disagree with me, but if I know the criticism comes from someone who *loves* me, I can look at it more objectively and accept it without retaliation. If a person loves me and has shown love to my family over the years, I know whatever he or she has to say is going to be in my best interest and I would do well to heed their advice. *"Love your enemies, do good to those who hate you"* (Luke 6:27).

We sometimes forget that churches are families too.

We sometimes forget that churches are families too. Just as in a biological family, there are going to be people in our churches who annoy us, whom we have a hard time getting along with and whom we may not trust or even like. Yet because we are a family in Christ, we must love them. Each time we come around the Lord's Table, we are coming together as a family around the "dinner table," showing again our commitment to Christ and to one another. We may differ on politics, solutions to global warming, and which football team to support, but we are all attached as branches to the Vine. His love is flowing through our veins.

> When I am hard to get along with, I have brothers and sisters who will not desert me. When my views seem strange or wrongheaded, they will still love me. When I make choices that leave them shaking their heads, they will not disown me. We are bound together by something that runs deeper than our likes and dislikes, our similarities and dissimilarities, our agreements and disagreements. We are joined by a reality that empowers us to transcend our differences enough to truly love one another...It is only here that we can ever find a fully satisfying and lasting answer to our own hunger to be safe, understood, and cared for—in the shared life created by the divine life we share.
> —*Praying with the Anabaptists*, Marlene Kropf and Eddy Hall

It is comforting to know that as we manage to love those so very different from us others are managing to love us even though we are so very different from them!

Peter gave us an important truth: *"Above all, continue to love each other deeply, because love covers a multitude of sins"* (1 Peter 4:8 ISV). Some translations describe it as a fervent love towards one another. This is more than having kind thoughts or wishing others well; this is deliberate, concerted, sacrificial effort on other people's behalf.

The aspect of love covering sins is also very important. Of course, the blood of Christ covers our sins. He pays the debt we owe. *"How blessed are those whose iniquities are forgiven and whose sins are covered! How blessed is the person whose sins the Lord will never charge against him!"* (Romans 4:7–8).

Experiencing God's Love in the Church

Think of it this way, too. We cover for each other—in good times and bad—our needs, our faults, our flaws. I once met someone for lunch at a restaurant and suddenly realized I had forgotten my wallet. My friend said, "Don't worry, I've got you covered." He was saying, "I'll take care of you" or "Let me be responsible for what you owe." Covering means to watch over people, to care for them when they are in need.

"I've got your back" is a similar phrase I love to hear. It means you can go into battle knowing there are those behind you watching out for you, who will give their lives to ensure nothing will come at you from an unexpected place. This gives people great confidence, because they know they are not alone; they know they have the support and encouragement of others carrying them forward. Unfortunately, too often Christians who venture out into challenging ministry do not find the church willing to "hold the ropes" or "watch their back." Instead they become victims of friendly fire!

This happens all the time in churches as members criticize and backbite each other. Sometimes an outsider can best point out flaws we tend to ignore, so that's why I'd like to share with you the thoughts of Liu Zhenying, known to his friends as Brother Yun. He was born in 1958, the fourth of five children, in a traditional farming village in the southern part of China's Henan Province. Both his salvation story and the way God raised him up to become one of the leaders of the home church movement in China are miraculous. He endured several imprisonments, torture, and life-threatening situations as God used him incredibly to spread the gospel message in his home country.

When he at last escaped from prison in China and made his way to the West, he thought he was free from persecution and hardship. But he was wrong. He simply faced a new kind of persecution: that of criticism, character assassination, ridicule, slander, and rejection.

In The Heavenly Man, he writes, "In China I had been used to beatings, torture with electric batons, and all kinds of humiliation...I guess that deep in my heart I had presumed that now

I was in the West my days of persecution had ended. In China, Christians are persecuted with beatings and imprisonment. In the West, Christians are persecuted by the words of other Christians."

Everybody Needs Grace

I have had the privilege of experiencing a variety of cultures in many different countries around the world. But sometimes I come across situations in churches that are perplexing and disturbing to me. During a speaking tour in southern India, a young church leader asked me a very disconcerting question. He wondered what his church should do to a teenage girl who had deeply embarrassed her family by becoming pregnant after being brutally raped. He wanted to know if she should be quietly expelled from the church or if her sins should be publicly denounced. Her parents were mortified that their daughter was carrying the results of someone's sin; particularly in that culture it brought great shame to the entire family. I suggested the church should offer support, encourage-ment, love, and compassion to this girl who had been a victim of a violent crime. But the man seemed confused and almost disori-ented by the idea that the church is to be a place of healing where those living with the consequences of sin—both the sinner and the sinned against—can find wholeness, grace, and redemption.

Christ's love often came in conflict with His culture as well. In John 8, His culture demanded the woman caught in adultery should be stoned to death, but love saved her life and gave her a second chance. In John 4, Christ's love broke several cultural barriers to spend time with a Samaritan woman. His love caused Him to heal on the Sabbath (Matthew 12). Christ's command to love transcends culture.

As difficult as it may be sometimes, the church as a whole must demonstrate what love looks like in practical terms.

■ Will they offer grace and forgiveness to those who have sinned or will they cast them out because they don't measure up to certain standards and expectations?

Experiencing God's Love in the Church

- Will the leaders show love to their critics and compassion to their detractors?

- Will the leaders walk humbly with the weak and discouraged or will they abandon them to find their own way back to the pathway?

Jesus said, *"You are my friends if you do what I command you. I do not call you servants anymore, because a servant does not know what his master is doing. But I have called you friends, because I have made known to you everything that I have heard from my Father"* (John 15:14-15 ISV). As we act toward others with the heart of Christ, we are demonstrating that we are His friends. As we neglect others, harm others, or treat others with contempt, we are showing that we are, in fact, His enemies.

Ultimately, the roots of our love problem can be found in the weakness of our love for Christ and His body. When we neglect our own personal relationship with God, then we are not connected to the Head of the body, who is Christ. *"He is the head of the body, the church"* (Colossians 1:18). If we do not stay connected to Christ, it is impossible to be truly connected with His people (His body) either. *"So we, being many, are one body in Christ, and individually members of one another"* (Romans 12:5). If love is to make a comeback in our churches, we must get back to the basics of prayer, spending time in His Word, valuing people more than programs, treating each other as family, and extending grace.

If we do not stay connected to Christ, it is impossible to be truly connected with His people.

■ ■ ■

The world's ways, methods, and values
have crept into our churches and are too often
wreaking havoc on unsuspecting people.

■ ■ ■

Chapter 6

Love Mistaken

The world's ways are not God's ways. *"Do not love the world or the things in the world. If anyone loves the world, the love of the Father is not in him"* (1 John 2:15). Some churches believe they have to copy the ways of the world to run their church organization. They somehow think a business model and popular corporate mantras will work in the body of Christ. The only problem is that the world's ways are often ruthless, heartless, uncaring, and cold—not what you want in God's church! The corporate model tends to casually set aside our Lord's command to love our neighbors as ourselves. What happened to the idea that they will know we are Christians by our love?

The world's ways, methods, and values have crept into our churches and are too often wreaking havoc on unsuspecting people. Let me share this true story. A church hired a local Bible college student as a summer youth worker. He believed the work experience would be useful in ministry after he graduated. This job was also his only income, and he planned to use what he saved to pay his final year's tuition in the fall.

The youth worker had a few disagreements with some parents over the course of the summer, but nothing that couldn't be worked out—or so he thought. At the end of the summer, he went to the church treasurer to receive his promised stipend, but he was told that there would be no money forthcoming as his job performance was unsatisfactory. The treasurer said he was sorry, but there was nothing he could do. The young man went to his car not knowing how he could even put gas in it, much less pay the tuition that was due in two weeks. He contacted his home church who scrambled and scraped the money together to cover his tuition costs.

When I was told this story by the college student, who is now a respected and admired associate pastor in a 15,000-member church, I was incensed and demanded to know the name and location of the church in order to confront them with this injustice. But the young man refused to tell me and said he learned a great lesson about God's people (his home church treated him with love; the other did not) and about depending upon God to take care of his needs. *"All that is in the world—the lust of the flesh, the lust of the eyes, and the pride of life—is not of the Father but is of the world"* (1 John 2:16).

> You cannot achieve the will of God by using the ways of the world.

Even in the case of moral failure, illegal activity, or inappropriate behavior, the goal should be biblical restoration, not vengeance or punishment for punishment's sake. Even in the face of obvious and egregious sins, the church is still entrusted with the ministry of reconciliation and forgiveness as painful as it may be to do so. You cannot achieve the will of God by using the ways of the world. Spiritual results are obtained through spiritual means, not through worldly methods or strategies.

In this chapter I examine some counterfeits to love—attitudes that have crept into our churches effectively squeezing out true Christian love from our midst.

Loving with the Wrong Motives

Have you ever received love with strings attached? Have you ever given love with strings attached? I've known people who've given money to churches in order to gain power and control. And it's no secret that people sometimes give (or show love) to boost their own pride, assuage their guilt, gain glory, impress their friends, manipulate others—the list could go on.

> Unfortunately our serving is sometimes tainted with our own self-interests, our need to impress others, or our desire to control people. Jesus asks us to serve as he served—with a heart overflowing with love, making no demands, simply offering the free gifts of grace.
> —*Praying with the Anabaptists*, Marlene Kropf and Eddy Hall

Love with strings attached is really not love at all. *"Now the purpose of the commandment is love from a pure heart, from a good conscience, and from sincere faith"* (1 Timothy 1:5).

A pastor once told me this story: His church wanted to minister to those in a nearby women's shelter. Food baskets were assembled, toys were collected for the children, and a gift was also purchased for each of the mothers. Members gathered together in a home to wrap and package the goodies and then delivered them to each of the broken families living at the shelter. Many of the recipients were astonished to find two gifts for each of their children and some for themselves. The baskets were dropped off without any pomp or fanfare, just the desire that they would know the love of God at Christmastime.

The next Sunday, they prepared a banquet for the same mothers and children to ensure they had a good Christmas dinner. The residents came with their children, happy and excited, and brought a thank-you card for the pastor with notes of appreciation to the church. The pastor told me that when he later read the card, tears came to his eyes as he noticed it was addressed to the church down the street!

He said to me, "Tom, at first I was disappointed, because I wanted our church to get credit for all that we did, but I realized that it was more important for God to get the glory than for us to get it. We didn't do all of this for us, we did it all for them."

True love comes with no strings attached.

Manipulation Is Not Love

Sometimes God's people try to manipulate God into doing things they want Him to do. We pray for things without even asking God first to see if He wants us to have them! We bargain with Him, make conditional vows to Him, even threaten to abandon Him if He does not come through for us. We should not be surprised when people who have no qualms threatening God seek to manipulate fellow church members as well. Whether it involves the finance committee or the pastoral search committee, property renovations or summer kids clubs, women's outreach teas or the nursery schedule, manipulating others to get one's way is a popular way to operate.

One particular manipulative tactic used in some smaller churches disturbs me. If the pastor wants to take the church in a particular direction but the wealthy families disagree with him, they "designate" their tithes or weekly offerings to specific budget items (such as religious education materials, youth ministry, summer camp scholarships, community outreach, etc.) thereby preventing their money from going into general funds. As a result, there is no longer enough money to pay the pastor's salary. If the pastor decides to comply with their demands, their tithes are then redirected back into the general account to pay his wages. This is sin, folks, plain and simple.

> I'm sure His heart is breaking as He watches how some of His people treat one another.

A few years back I heard of a group of church members who actually brought a lawsuit against their church leaders to force the church to go in a particular ministry direction. After many months of agonizing trauma played out within the church and in the media, the courts decided against this group. The rest of the church retaliated by removing these manipulative members from the membership rolls. Is this the way the church for which Christ died is supposed to act? Sue one another, take those to court who disagree with you, slander and trash-talk those who don't let you have your way? I'm sure His heart is breaking as He watches how some of His people treat one another.

Authoritarianism Is Not Love

Years ago I had a disturbing experience while working in a summer ministry position. The church's pastor decided we would all hand out fliers on a Sunday afternoon to promote a children's program beginning the next morning. I mentioned to someone in the office that I didn't know how I felt about "working" on Sunday. I was too young and naive to know my colleague would immediately go to the pastor to inform him of my concern. Rather than addressing my concern, the pastor told me I was fired for disloyalty and for questioning his authority. This was particularly disconcerting because I was the one in charge of running the kids program that started in the morning!

Far too many leaders in the church have not understood or grasped the concept of servant leadership. They don't understand what love should look like when working with volunteers in the church. Good and effective volunteers have left places of ministry disillusioned, angry, and bitter, vowing never again to serve because of how certain church leaders have treated them. *"Inasmuch as you did it to one of the least of these My brethren, you did it to Me"* (Matthew 25:40) constantly rings in the back of my mind.

Why is control so important to so many people? What is gained by wielding power in the church? Is it that people just love to see others doing things their way? Is it that they hate to take orders from anyone else? Is it that they alone presume to have all the right answers and best solutions to all the challenges the church faces?

What does Christ say about this?

As the Lord's servant, you must not quarrel. You must be kind towards all, a good and patient teacher, gentle as you correct your opponents.
—2 Timothy 2:24–25 (GNT)

Jesus sat down, called the twelve disciples, and said to them, "Whoever wants to be first must place himself last of all and be the servant of all."
—Mark 9:35 (GNT)

"And if one of you wants to be first, he must be your slave."
—Matthew 20:27 (GNT)

None of you should be looking to your own interests, but to the interests of others.
—1 Corinthians 10:24 (GNT)

Too often leaders have convinced themselves that they are serving God and doing what is right for the people, even though they leave others hurt, frustrated, disillusioned, and angry wherever they go. No one likes to be manipulated. No one likes to have their ideas and suggestions squashed every time they bring something up. And few people enjoy having someone breathing over their shoulder checking to make sure that everything is done just like the "boss" wants it to be done.

When one person or a small group of people controls the church, Christ no longer does. Think about this: If anyone is "in control" of the church, they have wrested it away from Christ and they are now leading according to their own agenda, with their own power, with their own wisdom and strength—and are unable to accomplish what God has in mind for His church. They cannot succeed in God's eyes. Even Christ, with all of His wisdom, power, and strength did not presume to function apart from His heavenly Father.

> *Then Jesus answered and said to them, "Most assuredly, I say to you, the Son can do nothing of Himself, but what He sees the Father do; for whatever He does, the Son also does in like manner."*
> —John 5:19

> *"I can of Myself do nothing. As I hear, I judge; and My judgment is righteous, because I do not seek My own will but the will of the Father who sent Me."*
> —John 5:30

> *Then Jesus said to them, "When you lift up the Son of Man, then you will know that I am He, and that I do nothing of Myself; but as My Father taught Me, I speak these things."*
> —John 8:28

Jesus' life, His every move, was in obedience to the Father. He submitted His will to the Father.

> The Christian life, like the life of Jesus on earth, is a combination of waiting and activity, or prayer and service. Jesus spent time alone with the Father in solitary places and then went forth in power to face incredibly busy days of ministry to needy people. Likewise, we must balance all our activities *for* him with time spent *with* him, waiting in expectant prayer and worship.
> —*Fresh Power*, Jim Cymbala

Although "all authority in heaven and on earth" was given to Jesus, He did not flaunt it or abuse it. He served His disciples and washed their feet. And He actually gave His power away to others and empowered them to accomplish amazing and incredible feats. *"Then He called His twelve disciples together and gave them power and authority over all demons, and to cure diseases. He sent them to preach the kingdom of God and to heal the sick"* (Luke 9:1–2).

Micromanaging Is Not Love

Micromanagers are people who have serious trust issues. These controllers, and that probably includes most of us at one time or another, have trouble believing people are capable of functioning on their own without their help. In the church, this means people are denied the opportunity to properly exercise their spiritual gifts or be led by the Holy Spirit to accomplish their tasks.

Micromanaging can take the form of a do-it-all, my-way-or-the-highway pastor, deacon, or other church leader. It also can be a suspicious congregation enlisting a staff member to spy on the senior pastor's every move (really). Often it is more subtle. Controlling people try to do the work of the Holy Spirit. So, rather than praying God would guide others, they pick up the phone to make sure these other people are doing their jobs properly. Rather than asking for God's power and wisdom and grace when interacting with people, they instead are predisposed to manipulate, irritate, bug, bother, and exasperate everyone around them. How can people learn and grow if someone is always telling them how to do things or forcing them to do things his or her way instead of allowing those people the freedom to learn to follow God and make decisions as He leads. There is no need to pray over things; just ask the committee chairperson what he or she wants done! Ridiculous.

Love invests in people and allows them to grow and develop their ministry skills. There should be a sense that even if a person fails or makes a mistake, there is plenty of grace to cover it and help them go on. God is not so much concerned with a perfect product as He is with the process of developing one of His children.

Again, Jesus empowered His disciples and sent them out. He did not spy on them to see if they were using His power correctly or if they were healing people in the exact same way He would have done. He trusted them to use His power wisely and in the best interests of others. He wanted them to experience the joy of seeing the Spirit of God work through them and the privilege of watching God bless their ministries as they obeyed Him.

Christ trusts His people with the responsibility of taking the gospel message to a waiting world, even with all of our flaws, fears, and failures. *"'I am telling you the truth: those who believe in me will do what I do—yes, they will do even greater things, because I am going to the Father'"* (John 14:12 GNT). The Great Commission is entrusted to us, with the eternal destinies of millions at stake, and yet the pastor or deacon or chairperson or congregation can't trust a committee to choose a carpet color for the foyer or what menu items should be served at the Valentine's banquet!

Love invests in people and allows them to grow and develop their ministry skills.

Love is often confused with control. Guiding someone is also not the same as controlling someone. Control takes the power away from others and does not give them the freedom to take responsibility for or even have the chance to learn from their possible failures. God lovingly gave us the freedom to explore our abilities and interests and to grow and learn on our own. He could have controlled His creation in such a way as to preclude the possibility of sin or failure, but He did not. He loves us and we can freely love Him in return. We can sin, repent, and be reconciled to Him. Controlling others is not loving them; it is putting them into bondage, taking their freedom away, and risking that others will resent you rather than love you.

My wife and I have a goal of raising our kids to be responsible, respectful, cooperative, helpful, and conscientious. So if we passed by one of their bedrooms to find Sunday's clothes in a pile on the floor, overdue homework assignments still on their desk, or mostly eaten food left on a plate on their dresser, we know we must address the situation. We have a choice: we can blow up at them or guide them more calmly toward the goal. I could barge into their room saying something like, "This room is an absolute disaster! You are such a slob. You cannot treat your dress clothes this way and expect us to give you anything new, and bugs are going to infest this pig sty with all this rotting food lying around! It is furthermore unacceptable for your homework to be late anymore. Look, if you cannot abide by the rules of this house and take better care of the things we give you, you might as well move out and find a place on your own!" But if I respond that way, I will damage my relationship with my son or daughter and only get reluctant compliance if and when he or she decides to do something about it.

The alternative would be to casually look into his room and say something like, "I see you have had trouble keeping your room clean this week and getting your homework done. It is suppertime, so just as soon as your room is picked up and clothes put away properly we would be happy for you to come and join us. And you can play your video games after all your homework is done, but not before," and then walk away. No anger, no name-calling. I want to treat my son with the same respect I would want him to show me, and I want us to maintain a good relationship. But I also have goals in mind that he is well aware of, and he sometimes needs reminding. We are not to bully, threaten, name-call, demean, or ridicule our children; neither should we treat any of our fellow church members in that manner.

Jesus told the famous parable of the prodigal son (Luke 15)—which some prefer to call the parable of the loving

> Controlling people lack such faith in God. Ultimately, their faith is in themselves alone.

father—in which a father had to choose whether or not to allow his younger son to receive his share of his inheritance. Withholding the money would have kept his son from squandering his hard-earned wealth. Many fathers would have done that, but the father chose to let him experience the good and bad of life. I believe the father must have spent many hours covering his rebellious son in prayer. The life lessons the son learned the hard way changed his heart and character forever. Controlling people lack such faith in God. Ultimately, their faith is in themselves alone. They cannot trust God, they cannot entrust others into God's hands, nor can they trust others to follow God's will or His ways without their direct, uninvited personal intervention.

Unforgiveness Destroys Fellowship

"Then Peter came to Him and said, 'Lord, how often shall my brother sin against me, and I forgive him? Up to seven times?' Jesus said to him, 'I do not say to you, up to seven times, but up to seventy times seven'" (Matthew 18:21–22). By asking the question, Peter showed he had every intention of offering forgiveness at least seven times, well beyond the call of duty! But Jesus almost reprimands him, and tells him an elaborate parable about an ungrateful servant (Matthew 18:23–35). The lesson of the parable is that forgiveness should not only be unlimited, it is also a requirement of God's kingdom.

For some reason, some people in the church choose not to forgive others, and they choose instead to hold grudges for years, even decades. They let petty offenses eat away at them and taint their relationships with fellow believers. The problem with this can be seen in the Lord's Prayer, which asks God to forgive us our sins, as we forgive those who have sinned against us (Matthew 6:12). We live in sin as long as we refuse to offer forgiveness to others. I suspect in most churches there are people teaching Sunday School, leading youth discipleship, singing in the choir, and playing the piano who are carrying around sin because they hold grudges against others. Unforgiveness is not permitted in God's kingdom of love, for love freely forgives all things. *"Therefore be merciful, just as your Father also is merciful. Judge not, and you shall not be judged. Condemn not, and you shall not be condemned. Forgive, and you will be forgiven"* (Luke 6:36–37).

Let me show you what this can look like in a church. Earlier, I mentioned the tragedy that befell Wedgwood Baptist Church in Fort Worth, Texas, in September 1999. When Larry Ashbrook entered the building, he did not come to worship or participate in student activities. He came to kill. Many people were shot that day and several died. Many more were terrorized and had their lives changed forever. But the church people were not the only victims that day; Larry's own family also suffered.

His parents and siblings were devastated over what he had done. Wedgwood's pastor, Al Meredith, and associate pastor, Mike Holton, soon visited the Ashbrook family to console them and offer immediate forgiveness. "They were hurting and just as horrified by it as we were," Holton told MinistryTodayMag.com ("Decade Later, Wedgwood Still Significant," September 12, 2009).

Over the next few years, Larry's brother Aaron received counseling and attended grief classes at various churches. He also periodically called on Meredith and annually visited the church in September around the anniversary of the shootings, bringing 14 roses in memory of those who were injured or killed. The members at Wedgwood have reached out to Aaron, even Kathy Jo Brown (now Rogers), whose husband was killed by Aaron's brother. Many have told Aaron that they consider him part of the Wedgwood family now, showing him that good can come out of darkness, according to Melody McDonald writing for the *Fort Worth Star-Telegram* ("Church Ravaged by Gunman Embraces His Brother," September 13, 2009).

Disunity Is Unloving

Disunity is not just the opposite of unity, it is anything less than complete unity. Some examples include:

- Conflicts that are not properly handled and resolved.

- Differences of opinion that people allow to divide them.

- Groups of people trying to outmaneuver others in order to get their way.

- Incessant criticism of others, including leaders.

- Withholding support for programs and ministries over minor issues.

- Vying for the attention of certain people of influence.

- Promoting some people (your friends) over others to positions of leadership.

- Redirecting church funds to pet projects over other worthy projects.

- Ganging up on people to silence their dissent or questioning.

- Leaders or others withholding information that the congregation has a right to know.

Look how Christ prays for unity among believers in His high priestly prayer recorded by the Apostle John:

"Now I am no longer in the world, but these are in the world, and I come to You. Holy Father, keep through Your name those whom You have given Me, that they may be one as We are."
—John 17:11

"I pray that they may all be one. Father! May they be in us, just as you are in me and I am in you. May they be one, so that the world will believe that you sent me. I gave them the same glory you gave me, so that they may be one, just as you and I are one: I in them and you in me, so that they may be completely one, in order that the world may know that you sent me and that you love them as you love me."
—John 17:21–23 (GNT)

It would appear that division was a common problem facing even the earliest churches. Paul urges believers to be united in heart and mind as they serve the Lord together. Throughout the Book of Ephesians he admonishes the believers to strive for unity. And listen to these words to other churches:

Brothers, in the name of our Lord Jesus the Messiah, I urge all of you to be in agreement and not to have divisions among you, so that you may be perfectly united in your understanding and opinions.
—1 Corinthians 1:10 (ISV)

Fill me with joy by having the same attitude, sharing the same love, being united in spirit, and keeping one purpose in mind.
—Philippians 2:2 (ISV)

Because they are united in love, I pray that their hearts may be encouraged by all the riches that come from a complete understanding of the full knowledge of the Messiah, who is the mystery of God.
—Colossians 2:2 (ISV)

We have to work to build and maintain unity in the body and not assume it will just happen because we are all Christians. In Paul's letter to the church in Philippi, he identifies an issue that

Experiencing God's Love in the Church

had come to his attention. He urges two faithful, godly, hard-working women to get along and to settle their quarrel (which is not specifically identified), and entreats a mutual friend to help them reconcile their differences. *"Euodia and Syntyche, please, I beg you, try to agree as sisters in the Lord. And you too, my faithful partner, I want you to help these women; for they have worked hard with me to spread the gospel"* (Philippians 4:2–3 GNT). Paul was well aware that when two people are quarrelling in the church, God's love cannot flow through them to others.

John said, *"If someone says, 'I love God,' and hates his brother, he is a liar; for he who does not love his brother whom he has seen, how can he love God whom he has not seen?"* (1 John 4:20). I wonder how many similar letters John or Paul could write to churches today asking people to get along! In a sense, they have written every church such a letter—we just need to heed the appeals the Holy Spirit made through them 2,000 years ago.

Why We Love

There are many different things that can prevent people from showing God's love to one another, and each of these things can be found in varying degrees in many churches today. It takes a very strong and concerted effort on the part of church members to preserve their love for one another and to protect the unity they have in Christ. I firmly believe that our adversary, the devil, would love nothing better than to see anything but love among God's people. Why? Look again at the prayer of Christ in John 17:

> *"I pray that they may all be one. Father! May they be in us, just as you are in me and I am in you. May they be one, so that the world will believe that you sent me. I gave them the same glory you gave me, so that they may be one, just as you and I are one: I in them and you in me, so that they may be completely one, in order that the*

*world may know that you sent me and that you love them
as you love me."*
—John 17:21–23 (GNT)

Did you catch the *"so that"* part? *"So that they may be completely one, in order that the world may know that you sent me
and that you love them as you love me."* The nugget of truth here
is that when church members do not show love to one another,
the world cannot properly know that
God loves them. Astonishing. If Christians within the church cannot show
love to one another, if they cannot be
of one heart and mind, if they cannot
get along, then a watching world will
never hear about God's love. Your
church might share the gospel with
these curious onlookers, but they will
not see the gospel in action. They will
not know the transforming power of God's love because there
will be no one to show them. The gospel will be words only and
no action. If it cannot be demonstrated among God's people,
then why would anyone believe it to be true? When we have no
love for one another, we render ourselves incapable of loving
not only non-Christians—but God as well.

When there's no love, it means the Spirit of God is not present either.

This is the most important reason for Christians to love one
another: it validates the reality of a living Christ, and it demonstrates the truth of the gospel. It shows the world that Jesus is
alive and well among His people because, as we have seen, loving one another is truly an act of God among His creation. In and
of ourselves it is nearly impossible to love those who come from
such varied backgrounds, different viewpoints, diverse cultures,
assorted personality types, and sundry tastes. But through God's
Spirit who lives in us, we are empowered to do it with joy. When
there's no love, it means the Spirit of God is not present either.
When that's the situation, all that is left for the church is judgment and impending doom.

Experiencing God's Love in the Church

We say "God is love," we can recite John 3:16, and we can quote the two greatest commandments about love. But when it actually comes to showing love to others, we often struggle. So, in the next chapters we will look at putting love in action. After all, where else can anyone find the love of God, if not in His church and among His people? If love cannot be found there, then there is no hope for a lost world. No hope at all.

■ ■ ■

That family invited Kim to lunch at a fast-food restaurant
after church. It wasn't a fancy meal, but it was much better
than eating a sandwich alone in her apartment.

■ ■ ■

Chapter 7

Love You Can See

In the spring of 1989, two years before we were married, my wife Kim was at a very low point. She had accepted a teaching position in a small town in Saskatchewan three years earlier in order to help plant a church in that community. Unfortunately, despite some success and much hard work, the church did not survive. Within the space of six months, Kim's closest friend moved away, a dating relationship ended, the pastor of the mission church and the pastor of the sponsoring church were both called to new assignments, and the church was unceremoniously disbanded.

Kim found herself alone and without a church family in a small prairie city. Confused and questioning God's plans for her life, Kim visited another church one Sunday. Hurting and angry at God and in no mood to worship, Kim had few expectations. When she arrived, the usher greeted her, asked her name and then, to Kim's surprise, introduced her to a family to sit with. That family invited Kim to lunch at a fast-food restaurant after church. It wasn't a fancy meal, but it was much better than eating a sandwich alone in her apartment. Over the course of the next few months that church began to show love to Kim in many ways. One family offered to pick her up and take her to a weekly Bible study with them, which became a tremendous source of support. Kim was later to learn that this family didn't normally attend this Bible study and went far out of their way to help her become involved. Also, they invited her to become involved in the church's music ministry despite the fact that they already had an ample supply of keyboard players.

This church made use of "encouragement cards" to give to one another to show appreciation for the ministry and service they gave to the church. Almost every Sunday someone would slip Kim an encouragement card and let her know they were praying for her. Numerous times Kim was invited into their homes for meals, which meant so much to a single person living in a small town.

After a year Kim accepted a teaching position in a different city, but was able to tell that congregation that their love and care for her had enabled a "wounded soldier" to get back in action. That church truly understood how to love the people God sent them. Thus far, we have explored some of the church's failings, and we've seen Christ's perfect example of love in action, but how does this apply in practice to the church right now?

Do Something Practical

> *"I was a stranger and you did not take Me in, naked and you did not clothe Me, sick and in prison, and you did not visit me."*
> —Matthew 25:43

If nothing else, love must be practical. Love does more than merely see a need, love seeks to *address* that need in tangible ways. Love does more than make plans of action, it actually *takes* action. It is always more than a feeling; it is a feeling that leads to actual involvement in the lives of others. The body of Christ, the church, is the one avenue through which God's love flows to a hurting world.

We alone, the men and women of the church, are called to this task, which has eternal consequences. We know that the earth and all of creation are dear to our Lord as *"All things were made through Him, and without Him nothing was made that was made"* (John 1:3). I know it is important to save the forests of the world, to reduce greenhouse gases, to watch over endangered animals, and to practice conservation and reduce waste whenever and wherever possible. We are to be good stewards over that which God has placed us in dominion. Greed, gluttony, selfishness, arrogance, and excess have plagued humanity from the beginning and will always tempt us towards unwise actions and choices. And I am sure God is grieved over the destruction mankind has perpetrated on His creation.

However, as good as the earth, the plants, and animals may be, the Bible tells us that at some point, all of it will pass away. *"But the day of the Lord will come as a thief in the night, in which the heavens will pass away with a great noise, and the elements will melt with fervent heat; both the earth and the works that are in it will be burned up"* (2 Peter 3:10). It wasn't to the earth or the plants or the animals or the stars in the heavens that God chose to demonstrate His love; it was to fallen mankind. The Bible indicates there will be a second chance for the earth to be renewed and restored (2 Peter 3:13–14), but for the souls of men and women, there is only one opportunity for them to respond to God's love. The Son of God *"has come to seek and to save that which was lost"* (Luke 19:10). *"And as it is appointed to men to die once, but after this the judgment"* (Hebrews 9:27).

When I see the masses of people inhabiting the continents on which I have traveled, I see people whom Christ created for eternity—people who will have only a relatively short time on earth to respond to God's love. That's where we come in. Christ has entrusted into our hands the incredible privilege to demonstrate His love to those He has created for eternity.

Love in Plain Sight

What do you see when you go to church to worship each week? Perhaps physical buildings. Maybe people gathering together listening to the preacher. People offering prayers to God, singing songs, collecting offerings. Perhaps you even see people gathering afterward and chatting over coffee. But do you see love?

It is my belief that there is nothing more pressing on the heart of God than for His people to show love to one another and to their friends, neighbors, and, yes, even their enemies. Love must be visible, or at least the effects of love should be evident. After visiting so many churches in my travels I feel I can get a sense of whether or not love is present almost as soon as I walk through the doors of the church, and sometimes even while I'm still in the parking lot.

I watch to see if people seem to genuinely enjoy being with one another.

I watch to see how the children and teenagers are treated. I watch to see how the elderly are accommodated. I look to see if the pastor is visible among the congregation before and after the services. I also look to see how long people fellowship together after the service has concluded. I watch to see if people seem to genuinely enjoy being with one another.

I've been told that most people need five to seven points of personal contact to feel welcome and accepted. That means they need a handshake, a conversation, a pat on the back, a shot in the arm, a hug, a nudge as they walk by, a positive comment, and in some cultures a kiss on both cheeks! For children, it means looking them in the eyes, grabbing their hand to give it a friendly shake, and possibly slipping a candy into their pocket as they pass by. Even a raised eyebrow or making a funny face can let a child know they are important, valued, and loved. This is not just the pastor's or staff's responsibility, it's everyone's opportunity.

Experiencing God's Love in the Church

Jesus told His disciples, *"Let the little children come to Me"* (Matthew 19:14). If a church truly values and loves children, there will be lots of families present. As a pastor, I tried my utmost to connect with every child and teenager who entered the church. I positioned myself in strategic locations at church so that children had to pass by me at some point. Do not underestimate how important it is to the fatherless child to have positive affirmation and attention from a caring, godly man at church. During my seminary days and later as a youth pastor, I worked with children's clubs and always made sure the ones without dads at home or the ones who felt neglected by their absent fathers were given an extra measure of attention and affirmation. Some children do not feel their church experience is complete until they have been teased, tussled, or acknowledged in some way by their pastor. It was a personal goal of mine to make our church a place where children enjoyed coming, where they had friends, and where they felt valued and loved. One of the reasons we attend our current church is because its members paid attention to our kids and went out of their way to encourage them and make them feel welcome.

Are you aware of how the children and teenagers are treated in your church? Are they quickly ushered out of the services so as not to disturb the grown-up worship? Do the teenagers have some space of their own in which they can gather and learn about the Lord? Does the church honor and publicly recognize the achievements of the youth and celebrate with them? I hope so. Never forget that these youth one day will be leading your pastor search committee or serving as board members and deacons. If you expect them to listen to your concerns when they are in positions of leadership, begin listening to their concerns now. One day, they will love you and treat you just as you have been treating them now.

Heaven forbid going to church should ever be drudgery, or some religious duty to be done! Going to church should be like going to a family gathering where cousins and uncles and aunts are there to let you know how special and important you are to them. It has to be a family of faith brothers and sisters in Christ coming together, celebrating God's goodness together. For my three children, church was always a fun place to go. I never had to threaten them to get up, cajole them to get dressed and have breakfast, or badger them to get into the car on time to leave for church. I can honestly say I have never had to fight with my kids to go to church because they have always looked forward to going to see their friends and family.

Love Notices What Others Miss

"My little children, let us not love in word or in tongue, but in deed and in truth" (1 John 3:18). What does it mean for a church to love in deed and in truth?

As a young boy, I still remember a gruff, old, white-haired gentleman whose clothes always smelled a bit musty. Mr. Abriel walked with a cane and sported a bushy, white moustache. Without fail, every time I saw him, he quietly reached into his suit pocket and pulled out a spicy licorice hard candy. I think they were called Humbugs. I can't recall ever having a conversation with him. I never saw him help with the kids ministry, and I don't remember seeing him and his wife in our home. But I remember how it felt to be noticed and quietly shown kindness by an elderly, respected member of the church, particularly as I hadn't any grandparents around. And, when you are one of five children in a family it is often difficult to get an adult's attention. He died only a few years later, but an impression was seared into my heart for what a church family could be like. And yes, I still carry an ample supply of small candies in my suit pocket or computer bag to give away to children. Of course, "sugar-free" candy is a good alternative to keep parents happy and limit hyperactivity!

It is no easy task for parents to raise children, particularly teenagers. Every parent faces power struggles, competing viewpoints, dueling priorities, and unexpected challenges along the way. But I can tell you it has been tremendously encouraging for me to watch other men and women taking time to talk to my teenagers at church. My kids get invited to use their musical skills on the praise team, to "hang out" with other teens in their homes, and some even take time out of their busy schedule to show up at my son's basketball games to cheer him on! All of these things are love in action. Love chooses to engage other people, to take an active interest in their lives and to go out of the way to encourage and support them. Sometimes love means striking up a conversation with a teenager dressed head-to-toe in all black and sporting weird jewelry in the strangest places. After all, he or she *did* come to church, whether under protest or not, and that young person needs to know that other people *want* them there and are interested in knowing who they are and what is important to them.

The hurting are another group of people to which a loving church will reach out; we can't afford to miss the opportunity to support them in their pain. I have been deeply moved when I've seen churches gather around hurting people to pray for them and to cry with them. I once spoke at a church in Ohio on the topic of my book, *The Family God Uses*. At the end of the service, a distraught woman came to the front of the auditorium and knelt down to pray. She was sobbing her heart out. I learned later that her family had been through tragedy after tragedy in the past months, and her heart was broken. She came to the one place she knew she could find solace. As she cried out to God in her anguish, one person, then another, then a few more began to slip out of their seats and quietly walk up to sit beside her on the floor and place their arms on her shoulder. Some whispered prayers for her, some who knew her circumstances cried with her, and others just let their supportive presence be felt. The church was not going to allow this woman to go through her pain alone. Her "family" was going to walk with her during this time of pain and grief.

Love Practices Hospitality

Let's look at a biblical imperative: hospitality. The English word is a translation of a Greek word, *philoxenia*, which means "love of strangers." Where some translate this word as "hospitality" others translate it as "welcome strangers in his home." In the context of the early church, travelers or visitors may have come from great distances, or at least other parts of the country. Church members would welcome and often provide a place for them to stay and food for them to eat. This was normal, and it was expected. The disciples were indignant after Christ sent them to find accommodations in a Samaritan village, because they were refused hospitality by the local people (Luke 9:53). Christ expects His people to be generous and kind and to treat others as they would want to be treated.

Paul knew much about this as he received hospitality from others on numerous occasions throughout his ministry. Peter likely did too. Listen to some of what the New Testament says:

> *Not lagging in diligence, fervent in spirit, serving the Lord; rejoicing in hope, patient in tribulation, continuing steadfastly in prayer; distributing to the needs of the saints, given to hospitality.*
> —Romans 12:11–13

> *Let brotherly love continue. Do not forget to entertain strangers, for by so doing some have unwittingly entertained angels.*
> —Hebrews 13:1–2

> *A church leader must be without fault; he must have only one wife, be sober, self-controlled, and orderly; he must welcome strangers in his home; he must be able to teach.*
> —1 Timothy 3:2 (GNT)

> *Open your homes to each other without complaining.*
> —1 Peter 4:9 (GNT)

One of the requirements for leadership in the church is to be hospitable, to be quick to welcome strangers. According to the Apostle Paul, if you are not willing to have people in your home, you are not qualified to be a leader in your church. This is a simple courtesy, a gesture of kindness and of friendship, not an inconvenience or hardship! In so many churches today this simple courtesy seems to have become a threat to people's very way of life. There are so many excuses people make for why they are unwilling to show hospitality not only to newcomers and visitors but also members that they have known for years. Their house might not be clean. They wouldn't know what to cook. They don't know if there is enough food in the house. They think they are not very good at "entertaining." Perhaps visitors would be allergic to their cats. Sunday is their day of rest. They just don't have company over to their place. So they wave good-bye to Jesus and leave Him standing alone in the foyer at church. *"Then they will reply, "Lord, when did we see you hungry or thirsty or as a stranger or naked or sick or in prison and didn't help you?" Then he will say to them, "I tell you with certainty, since you didn't do it for one of the least important of these, you didn't do it for me""* (Matthew 25:44–45 ISV).

> The essence of hospitality is opening up your life to others.

The essence of hospitality is opening up your life to others, particularly those who are strangers and new to the community. It's lonely and intimidating to be a newcomer to any group. Extending an invitation to share in the life of your family is an expression of the love of Jesus.

We must put the erroneous notion away that we are trying to impress others, or show off our house, or astonish them with our cooking. Hospitality is about letting other people into our life and our home—not putting on a show for them. Put hot dogs and macaroni and cheese on my dinner plate and I am happy!

People want someone to care for them, not impress them with their antique collection or culinary expertise! A simple, "Come as you are to see us as we are" is sufficient.

It is such a shame that so many people are too intimidated to show kindness to strangers and visitors. Hospitality can happen by simply including others in your family's everyday activities. Invite others to join your family at a casual restaurant after church or on a family outing. It need not require labor-intensive preparations. Think outside the Martha Stewart box! Jesus wants us to care enough to include a newcomer and let him or her become a part of our church family.

> People want someone to care for them, not impress them with their antique collection!

I think most of us are not hospitable enough, but let me add a word of caution here as some of you may have been burned by welcoming unscrupulous strangers. Love and trust are *not* the same thing. Trust is earned; love is given freely. I would welcome a stranger into my home, but never leave them alone with my children or my valuables! I can love a stranger but might not loan them my car, because I have no basis upon which to think they are a safe driver. Don't be foolish. It is all right to set limits for the protection of people and property. Love does not mean you are a doormat to pushy people; it does not mean you are always the one to pay for lunch; and it does not mean you always loan things to people who will not take care of them properly. You can protect yourself and set boundaries around your family and home while loving others.

Love Thinks Outside the Box

I recently met an intriguing young family at a conference in southern Texas. They sat across the table at the church dinner that evening and their young daughter sat next to me. She and I became instant friends as she reminded me a great deal of my daughter at a younger age. There were two young boys with them as well. One of them looked quite different from the rest of the family. Over the next day and a half, I learned their story. There was a grandmother in this young mother's Sunday School class who was trying to raise a grandson with great difficulty. This lad had been abandoned by his drug-addicted mom and a father who was in prison for killing his father-in-law. The grandmother was no longer physically or emotionally able to raise the boy and wanted to retire to a city several states away. Her story pierced the heart of the young mother who shared with her husband what she felt God wanted her to do. This boy had witnessed the death of his grandfather, seen his mother abuse drugs, watched his alcoholic and abusive father go to prison for murder—and now knew his grandmother no longer wanted him.

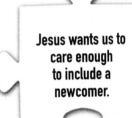

Jesus wants us to care enough to include a newcomer.

After much prayer, this young couple determined to open their home to this ten-year-old boy. They described to me the challenges they faced by adding him to their family, but I could see in their eyes the growing love they had for this boy as he opened his heart to them in return.

Love Brings a Casserole

Have you heard of the casserole ministry? Well, if you've been on the receiving end of it, you will understand what a difference it makes. During times of need, such as the birth of a child or a parent in the hospital or extended illness, the head of the casserole ministry (or a Sunday School teacher or small group leader) arranges with others to provide the family a week's worth of dinners, delivered once a day for seven days. In my experience, the main dish was often twice as much as a family needed, so the meals were stretched out for nearly two weeks with leftovers. When my wife had pneumonia for several weeks, our doorbell would ring about five o'clock, and there was a demonstration of love standing on our doorstep with several bags of ready-to-eat dinner. You should have seen the excited looks on my three children's faces as we dived into the bags discovering what wonderful and delectable surprises awaited us. There was also relief on their faces that Dad was not going to have to cook that night.

Love Gets Involved

Sometimes love goes beyond a casserole. Love gets involved in the lives of hurting and needy people—people in crisis—even if it gets messy.

Helping the mentally ill.
In the churches I have served, there have always been people who suffer from mental illness. Several persons were bipolar, one had schizophrenia, and others suffered with clinical depression. I am not a trained counselor, a psychologist, a psychiatrist, or a medical doctor. Often I felt totally inadequate as a pastor to deal with manic behaviors, but though we were not trained professionals, we were a church who loved our members. Maybe all we could do was to gather in the parking lot of the hospital and pray while our friend underwent electroshock therapy in an attempt to "reboot" her brain patterns (as I understood it). We also went to pick up a middle-aged man for church on a weekly basis knowing he would remain alone in the dark without eating all day if we didn't. On two separate occasions I requested that our church leaders interview one of these members so that they could help us help them when they were in the throes of their mental illness. We asked what it was like for them during a manic episode, or how it felt to go on the downward spiral of depression. We wanted to know what practical things we could do to help them and their families through these times. You have no idea just how appreciative our church leaders were to be able to have a better understanding of what these members

were going through and to have some practical steps to take in order to show our love and concern for them. You also should have seen the faces of these two dear members who, for the first time, could openly and honestly discuss their mental illness in a safe environment knowing these leaders intended to do more than gather information; they intended to be involved in the lives of their families from this point on. Love never quits, but finds a way to care.

Helping military families.
Some of our members at North Sea Baptist Church in Norway served at the local NATO base and were unexpectedly given notice of a three-month deployment to Bosnia. We immediately marshaled our members into action. Some members mowed lawns for young moms whose husbands had been deployed. Some took carloads of kids fishing on behalf of those dads who were missing fishing season with their children. I even got an email from one deployed husband who told me it was his wedding anniversary the next week and asked if I would help surprise his wife. I bought the flowers, the candy, and the card and dropped it off to her house one evening with his name signed on the card. I am not quite sure if she ever figured out how the gifts got on her doorstep. I began sending manuscripts of my weekly sermons by email to our deployed members so they could remain connected to their church family back home. I was told these sermons were printed and handed around among the troops! We also gathered our families together for a time of prayer when the news of the 9/11 attacks reached our people. Several of our members had colleagues at the Pentagon or working at the World Trade Center. It was significant that the local newspaper sent a photographer to our home and published a photo of our members praying for one another the next morning.

Helping those with urgent needs.
Members of our church in Norway provided financial counseling to other members and taught classes on how to develop a family

budget. Some made sure the cars and lawn mowers of financially-strapped members were always working. We purchased and installed a wood-burning stove for a widow on a pension. Other members made sure single moms with kids were always invited to their family dinners at Thanksgiving, Christmas, and Easter. Refugees in the church were given furniture and odd jobs to earn some money until they got on their feet. Teenagers kicked out by overbearing fathers were allowed to stay in a rent-free basement suite as a stopgap measure while others worked on reconciliation. I recall going to the house of a desperate, elderly gentleman who told us a fellow to whom he had given temporary shelter for the night was refusing to leave the next day. So I picked up the biggest deacon I could find and together we went to remove this man from the home and then monitored the situation over the next few days to ensure his safety. Love is not deterred by fear.

Love is not deterred by fear.

After reading these examples, what examples are you aware of in your own life or in the life of your church family that you can add to this list? It is so important to test whether or not you and your church love one another as Christ has loved you, because your words and good intentions are meaningless unless backed up by your actions.

Jesus demonstrated for His disciples (and us) what love looks like in the flesh. Of course, in the end, He demonstrated the ultimate act of love for us by dying on the Cross—something He had alluded to earlier during His ministry when he said in John 15:13, *"Greater love has no one than this, than to lay down one's life for his friends."*

If Jesus Came to Your Church Would He Come Back?

Showing love to your friends and your spiritual family should be easy to do. It should come naturally and with ease. But what do you do with the outsider or the stranger you find in your midst?

So far in this chapter we've looked at the love of Christ in action among those already in the church body. But Christ is also always building His church. There are two verses that should guide our thoughts every time

It is the Lord who adds people to His body.

we enter the fellowship: (1) *"And the Lord added to the church daily those who were being saved"* (Acts 2:47), and (2) *"Truly, I tell all of you with certainty, the one who receives whomever I send receives me, and the one who receives me receives the one who sent me"* (John 13:20 ISV).

It is the Lord who adds people to His body. If you see a new person or new family visiting your church, you have to assume God is up to something. It is important for us to be aware of those God is bringing into our church building and those who are getting involved in our various ministries, because God may be really trying to tell us something important. If God is adding a person or family to your church body, then He thought it was necessary for them to be added for your benefit and the benefit of the overall ministry of the church.

- What gifts are they adding to the body?

- What abilities does your church need that they have to offer?

- What resources do they have access to that match God's revealed will and direction for your church?

- What do they have to teach your church from their experience with God?

- How might they need your church to express love to them?

Moreover, the manner in which we treat the people God sends us is the manner in which we are treating Christ (Matthew 25:40). This verse is extremely important. If Christ came to our church, would we leave Him standing alone in the foyer while we chat with our friends? Would we look at His strange clothes and long hair and sit on the opposite side of the room from Him? Would we ignore Him altogether or make fun of Him because He is not familiar with the songs we sing? If Jesus came to your church, would He come back a second time?

My nephew went off to study in a new city and needed to find a church home. He did not know anyone in town and his family was a four-hour drive away. He was told one large church had lots of activities for college kids, so he went to check it out. Not wanting to miss anything, he walked in early to look around. A few young people greeted him, asked his name, and then went off to be with their friends. This happened for the next two weeks. People said hello, then left him standing alone.

On the fourth Sunday, he arrived early and found a seat in the middle of a pew waiting for the service to start. He watched as the entire row in front of him filled up with students. Then the entire row behind him became packed with students. During the greeting time, both rows on either side of him reached over him to shake the hands of their friends, but not one person went to sit with him or invite him to sit with them. He decided he would never arrive early again! He started to arrive after the service had started and slip in to the first empty seat he could find and would leave just before the service was over to avoid the disappointment and rejection. Eventually he left that church and found one where he was warmly invited into the college group and was given ministry responsibilities to lead worship among his peers. The pastor even invited him to lunch to welcome him to the city and find out how they could help him adjust. One congregation thought they were friendly, greeting and asking the names of the visitors, but they were not willing to open their hearts to him. The other brought him into their family and gave him a place to serve in ministry. Which one do you think showed love?

Think for a moment about what people see when they come to your church.

- What do they experience? What do they notice?

- What is evident to them about the way people interact with one another?

- Is it easy to navigate your ministries, facilities, and worship experience?

- How well does your church reflect and demonstrate the kind of love we have so far described?

- Do you view each person who visits your church as being sent by God on purpose?

- Do you treat newcomers as you would treat Christ?

- What percentage of people who visit your church return a second time?

We were created in the image of God, so at our core we were created to reflect the heart of God. There should be no surprise, then, to know that people look for and respond to love. It's been shown that children in orphanages who are picked up and held and shown love will thrive much faster and become much healthier than those who are shown little or no affection. People thrive when loved and deteriorate without it. The same is true in our churches.

One fellow who visited our church in Norway jokingly complained to me that it took him nearly 15 minutes to get to a seat on entering the building because so many people stopped him and introduced themselves, asking who he was and where he worked. Later that week, our members visited him and his family, and it was not long before they were involved in various ministries.

Would You Let Your Brother Just Walk Away?

I share this story as a warning to all of us. A family moved to a new community and began attending a church that, on the out-

"When we finally left the church, not one person called us."

side, was very friendly and appeared to have a lot going for it. But after more than a year, they observed that none of the church leaders or church families had made any effort to get to know them or bring them into the life of the church. After much prayer, they decided to look for another church to attend. Their desire as a family was to be integrally involved in the life of the church, not just to be observers kept at arm's length.

When a church staff member learned they were no longer attending, he asked to have coffee with them; some would call it an "exit interview." His stated intention was to help them "leave well." His desire was for them not to leave angry or bitter or with unresolved issues, but his statement hurt because they did not really want to leave at all; they simply wanted a church that would open their arms and love them. They did not want their children to grow up in a church that did not know how to show love to one another. Had the staff member been more concerned about helping them "stay well," he would not have had to help them leave well.

Leaving a church is never an easy thing to do. There is a lot of grieving, hurting, loneliness, and frustration involved. I have heard people say with deep sorrow over and over and over again, "When we finally left the church, not one person called us." Sometimes people leave because they don't think they are wanted or needed, and that idea is proven true when no one notices they are not coming back and no one calls to see where they are. I know that if my son or daughter walked away from our family because they were angry or hurt, I would chase them down and bring them back! I would tell them without any shadow of doubt that I love them and that they are important to our family. How can we let person after person walk away and have no one even call to check on them? I am sorry, but this is just a disgrace. So many churches need to seriously repent of letting brothers and sisters walk away without making any effort whatsoever to reclaim them and bring them back into the family.

I am sorry, but this is just a disgrace.

Steps to Closing the Back Door

What is your strategy for helping visitors return and stay in your church? Keep it simple. The bottom line is to love them. But here are some practical suggestions that many different churches have used with some success (and some may apply to your regular attendees and members as well). I share them to help you think of what you can do in your local body.

- Designate certain members (without "greeter" badges) to watch specifically for visitors each week in order to connect with them immediately before and/or after the worship service. If you use visitor cards, make sure the information is correctly filled out and that the visitors know they are appreciated and welcome to come back again anytime.

- Sensitize your congregation to whom God may bring to your church each week and encourage your people to make an effort to chat first with visitors and with their friends second.

■ Visitors often are the first ones to leave when the service is over, so most people may not even notice the visitors leaving. Designate people who will stand near the exit doors to be sure visitors have been identified, welcomed, and offered a visit by staff or members during the week. Ask them to be sure they have filled out an information card prior to leaving for immediate follow-up by staff a few days later.

■ Plan to visit in the home of visitors within a week or so, if not less. The church staff does not have to visit first; any members who are enthusiastic about the church and can represent it well to newcomers would be great. Be sure to bring a thank-you gift from the church when you go, as well as an information packet about your church that includes a church history, church values, staff pictures and contact information, and information on the various ministries with contact information for newcomers to review. If your pastor or staff members have written books, offer one for free. During the visit, be sure to find out about their family, their background, their concerns, and their interests. If you have a coffee bar at church, give them a free coffee coupon to be used on their next visit.

■ For students especially, be sure to collect coupons (two-for-one meals, fast-food discounts, office supplies, movie passes, bus tickets, free coffee at the church coffee bar, etc.) for anything that would be practical and useful to them.

■ Have a monthly free lunch for any newcomers or visitors who have stopped by your church that month. Order in pizza and salad, show a brief presentation of your church, staff, and ministries, and then let your church leaders act as hosts at each table. Open the floor for questions. Make sure entire families are invited with personal email or telephone invitations.

■ Get visitors' email addresses or Facebook contact information and send them a note of appreciation for their attendance and offer to answer any questions they may have.

■ Send their teenagers text messages on their cell phones letting them know about upcoming youth events.

Remember, being friendly is not just greeting people and asking their names, it is asking them to sit with you and your family in church and perhaps go the extra mile and invite them to lunch afterwards. Visitors want to know if they can relate to the people at a new church. Members and visitors are looking for a church family where they belong and are accepted. They are looking to make connection with others, be spiritu-

> **Members and visitors are looking for a church family where they belong and are accepted.**

ally challenged, worship, pray, be discipled, given a chance to serve, and have a place where their children will be able to make friends.

"And for their sakes I sanctify Myself, that they also may be sanctified by the truth. I do not pray for these alone, but also for those who will believe in Me through their word that they may all be one."
—John 17:19–20

■ ■ ■

I believe one of the most valuable initial steps a church
can take on its journey back to love is to listen to those
who are in desperate need of love.

■ ■ ■

Chapter 8

Love Reclaimed

Loving God, you have baptized us into one body and made us to drink the one Spirit. Now grant us pure and faithful hearts that we may serve one another diligently in love and find no cause to separate or divide. Call each of us to esteem others better than ourselves so we may remain together in peace and joy. Grant these mercies to us and all your people. Amen.

—*Praying with the Anabaptists,* "Prayer of Tijs Jeuriaenss," Marlene Kropf and Eddy Hall

I believe one of the most valuable initial steps a church can take on its journey back to love is to listen to those who are in desperate need of love: the ill, the needy, the lost, the hurting. It is nearly impossible to guess what people think or how they feel unless we have been in their shoes ourselves. I'd like you to hear from a variety of people from different walks of life, and some people who minister among them, to gain some insights into what they see and feel when they come to church.

Perhaps you or one of your family members fall into one of the groups mentioned below, and maybe you will nod your head in agreement as you read. You may also have other suggestions or insights that could very well be included here. Let me recommend that you pray about taking time to help your fellow church members understand your situation and give them suggestions for ministering to those in need of love, which, ultimately, is all of us.

Just Ask

Churches and church members don't always know what to do or how they can help. Sometimes their efforts even do more harm than good. Well-meaning, good-intentioned people make mistakes all the time. When I learned that my sister was diagnosed with cancer—she was 16 at the time—I did not need people to quote to me Romans 8:28, *"all things work together for good,"* as some did. I needed someone to cry with me and to pray with me for my sister's recovery. Christians are not perfect. We need helpful, insightful strategies to show love; otherwise we may compound the problems that hurting people face.

> Churches and church members don't always know what to do or how they can help.

- Some people try to "rescue" those in need from their troubles while neglecting the reason they are in trouble in the first place.

- Others give people what they ask for rather than helping them find what they really need (for example, only giving someone money instead of helping that person find a job).

Experiencing God's Love in the Church

- Some lay guilt trips on hurting people for their life situation.

- Some help out with ulterior motives, and some nefarious people actually exploit needy people for their own benefit.

Even though the church is created in love and called to live in love, the people of God sometimes fail to live up to their heritage and calling. Individual congregations fail; so do individuals within the church. At such times, prayers of confession are necessary for cleansing, healing, and the emergence of new life.
—*Praying with the Anabaptists,* Marlene Kropf and Eddy Hall

This chapter is in no way meant to be an exhaustive list of the people in our churches who need to see Christ's love in action. I simply offer a representative sample of those who come through our church doors every week. Based on emails I received and interviews I conducted, below you will read their stories in their own words, or the stories of those who already minister among them.

CARING FOR THE DIVORCED OR SEPARATED
by Karen, a divorced mom

Separation and divorce are difficult situations in a church. We are told God hates divorce (which He does), but yet it still happens way too often. Not only are there many losses (children, extended family, finances, couple friends, home, lifestyle, identity, etc.), but there is a tremendous amount of shame involved.

People in church often don't handle this well. Perhaps they don't know who to support, because it may look like they are aligning themselves with one party over another. There may be a lack of mercy, because they think one or both parties must be to blame; perhaps they feel the outcome is deserved. Or maybe they are concerned that if they support the person, then they will be condoning the breakup of the marriage. Most often people just don't know what to do or say.

A grieving person makes many people uncomfortable. At times the most practical way to love someone is to let them know that you care for them, to sympathize with their pain, and to be there to talk to, if they want. Here are some suggestions for how to lovingly respond:

- A divorced or separated person often has continual thoughts about the situation that dominate his or her mind. They may need to talk about issues repeatedly. Ask questions and listen to what he or she has to say. There is no need to solve their problems or bash the other spouse. Most often, he or she just wants someone who will listen and care. Talking about the situation can often temporarily ease the pain just a bit. Divorce and/or separation is not an event; it is a long, difficult process with many struggles and challenges along the way before healing takes place and a new normalcy takes over.

- The church (pastor and members) should be in contact with both separated persons after the breakup. This can be a devastating and lonely time; they may not be stable. The actual extended family of the couple may be dealing with their own anger and hurt and unable to help properly.

- Send a card, call him on the telephone, or take her out for coffee. Pray with him or her.

- The pastor should ask to pray over or with the family. (I asked my pastors to do this, so that my children knew that they were being lifted up to God and being supported by the church.)

- Provide financial assistance, food, clothing, or other items, if you can. Help those moving to a new home.

- Women may need help initially with some of the things their husbands might have done. Some examples might be: regular vehicle maintenance, home maintenance (such as draining the water from outside pipes before the winter or changing furnace filters), putting up Christmas lights, learning to pay the bills, buying a car, or mowing the lawn.

- Men may need help at first learning to make balanced meals and school lunches, doing the laundry and the ironing, and caring for a sick child.

The more the church can meet the newly separated or divorced person's needs, the less likely that the person will seek out new or unhealthy relationships.

SUPPORTING MILITARY FAMILIES
by Lt. Col. Michael Husfelt, US Air Force Chaplain (from "Churches Reap Blessings from Military Ministry," Deacon *magazine, Summer 2010)*

Military families have many of the same needs as their civilian counterparts. They need a place to belong, a sense of community, and a welcoming place to worship. And, because they are often at an assignment for only two years or so at a time, they need ways to integrate quickly into the church body. They often face frequent relocations from one military assignment to the next, the uncertain duration of such assignments, and extended family separations due to deployments far from home (or training to prepare for such deployments). Churches should show appreciation and support for their military members, regardless of political differences or opinions on military policy or strategy.

Probably the best people in your church to minister to members of the military are those with current or prior service in the military themselves. Veterans have a heart for the needs of the military community, they understand military culture, and often have firsthand experience with the challenges frequent relocations bring to families. Veterans are an excellent resource in developing an ongoing ministry to military families in and around your church. Here are a few other recommendations for churches:

- Be practical. When a need arises (particularly during a deployment), church members can provide support for things like meals, respite childcare, auto or home maintenance issues, and lawn care. Make regular phone calls, send notes, and ask, "How can we help?" rather than "Call if you need something." Assume help is needed; don't wait to be called. The children of deployed parents are always looking for surrogate parents, grandparents, uncles, and aunts to fill in for relatives they may rarely see. Send care packages to those who are deployed. Offer driving lessons to teenagers. Or help kids develop athletic skills that their dads are not there to teach them, like hitting a baseball.

- Be prayerful. Pray for and encourage your military families. Regularly recognize and honor church members serving abroad and display their pictures while taking time to pray for their specific needs. Don't forget you can still have an impact on their spiritual life while they are deployed through your church Web site, by uploading sermons or Bible studies on the Internet, and by praying for them.

- Be collegial. If a military installation is nearby, make contact with the chapel staff. Express your desires and concerns and offer your support for the chaplain's community. Ask if there are specific needs or ways your church can support the chapel's ministry and the military community in your area.

- Be missional. Equip and encourage military families to live out their faith right where they live for however long they are able to live where they are. Love them where they are, pray for their assignment, and help them grow spiritually wherever they may be.

- Be patient. Don't pretend like nothing happened when they come back from an assignment. Let them know you are there for them and their family, and ask them to help you help them. Spend time one-on-one over lunch; give them open doors to walk through when they are ready to talk. Be a good listener rather than a good talker.

- Be sacrificial. Plan on using resources to bless military families in practical ways. You may need to offer financial assistance, your time, or your resources. Share your family with them. Plant seeds and expect God to bring the increase. Be sure to be there for the family's special events if Mom or Dad is out of the country (graduations, birthdays, concerts, driving lessons).

- Be kingdom-focused. Focus on the big picture and ask God to keep your heart tender for the worldwide church and missions field—not just local ministry.

Discipling and training military families will not only impact your current congregation, it will be a blessing that goes far beyond your local area as they move around the world! Your congregation's military members will be better ambassadors for God and their country if they have been loved, challenged, and commissioned by your church to live a life that honors Him for today and eternity. The seeds you sow in their lives will harvest a more secure peace for today and the lasting result will be a positive impact for eternity!

LOVING FELONS
by Christopher, a former federal prisoner

Prison is an ugly place. I know that I probably would not have survived my incarceration (from age 20 to 32) and life after release if not for God's presence.

A lot of the time, the road to prison begins in childhood. We come from broken homes, have parents who abuse drugs or alcohol, and all the rest that goes with that. There's a lack of structure, stability, love, and moral guidance in our youth and in our homes. By the time we end up in prison, we are often bitter, hurt, angry, depressed, and just plain mad. Mad because we feel we got a raw deal in life. We feel like outcasts or rejects. I found, during my time in prison, that most prisoners refuse to take responsibility for their choices and the actions that led to their incarceration. Time after time after time I saw prisoners blame their childhood, parents, spouses, skin color, etc., for the choices they made that put them behind bars. It was as if no one was willing to say, "Hey, I messed up."

The reason I am sharing this is because I truly believe that if a prison ministry is really to make some lasting changes, it must address taking responsibility for one's choices right alongside that responsibility of choice in accepting Jesus as Lord and Savior. That means past and future choices. We need to come to terms that we all are sinners. None of us are perfect, and we all have a major problem with sin.

The good news is we all have a major solution to our major problem: Jesus. But accepting Christ is not some magical mantra that will cause all our problems to go away or make life easier. Jesus solves our spiritual problem, and no doubt can solve any earthly problem. But that doesn't mean that it is God's will to do so at any given place and time. Many Christians still have problems even on a daily basis. I accepted Jesus, and to this day my life isn't easy. In fact, accepting Jesus can often cause even *more* problems as the lord of this world, the devil, comes against you to discourage you and try to discredit God.

"Let them see Jesus in you."

It would be good for churches doing prison ministry to have some kind of mentoring program for prisoners. This can start when they are still behind bars and continue after their release, offering them love and support before and after they reenter society. Believe me, it isn't easy being a Christian in prison. Most people don't realize how the love and compassion of even just one person in a prisoner's life can make all the difference. Don't hand them Jesus and walk away. They will look for the Jesus in you first of all. What they see or don't see in you will determine a lot. Let them see Jesus in you.

I know prisoners can be unpleasant. People were unpleasant to Jesus when He was here, but He still loved them. He still cared for them. When you go into a prison, understand the prisoners are hurting. Everything they took for granted has been taken away from them. They've been separated from loved ones, and many are utterly alone in a dark, dark place. Even though many feel they have to be tough just to survive, they are not heartless or beyond caring. When my mom died while I was in prison, I wept silently at night with my head under my blanket so as not to let my tears be seen by other prisoners.

A major problem I've witnessed is the failure of Christians to lovingly welcome the prodigals home. Even after release, we are still punished by society for being felons. It affects where we can live (most landlords won't rent to a felon), our ability to find employment, and our relationships, among many other things. Too often we are condemned and judged by those who are supposed to be our family in Christ. When people are trying to repent and live rightly with God, they need even more compassion, not less.

Dealing with Mental Illness

If you have not experienced mental illness, it is nearly impossible to understand fully what a person is going through. There are also so many aspects of various illnesses that to understand one does not mean you can understand another type of mental illness. From obsessive-compulsive behaviors to chronic depression, from multiple personality issues to bipolar chemical imbalances, the illnesses manifest themselves in different behaviors and require different types of responses by loving church members. But in every situation people battling mental illness need compassion, grace, love, and understanding. They will at times also need forgiveness, incredible patience, and someone who will never give up on them.

BIPOLAR DISORDER
by Wendy

I am doubly blessed. I embraced Christianity into my heart because of my illness. The struggles of dealing with bipolar disorder have resulted in growth and deeper friendship, partially due to a supportive church family. Christian individuals in my current church family and others that have touched me along my journey have made a difference when they first choose to know me, accept me, and embrace all of me in love as Christ commands. Not all members have reached out, but I do not feel shunned or rejected when I attend church. Acceptance as an individual by fellow Christians is vital. My long periods of balance between episodes allow people to get to know me in a stable state, which leads to a desire to support me through times of difficulty.

> "Being prepared for possible behaviors can make it easier to support people with mental illness."

I feel closest to those church members who are open to me. They do not just greet me in church and expect an answer that everything is fine. They welcome a true answer. When I feel comfortable, I share. Sometimes I am stressed and feeling unbalanced; other times I need prayer to deal with a specific situation. Even in times of stability I need support to keep my perspective and figure out how to "let go and let God."

I feel most loved by those who go beyond church chat. The visits outside of church are best. I bond most to those who invite me into their homes. We invite each other out to lunch. These friends are the ones I grow in Christ with. I have taken part in some great home groups where I felt loved and enjoyed socializing and growing together in Christ. As an individual with a mental illness, socializing with people from all walks of life is important. These types of groups have been vital to my state of remission.

Some individuals who struggle with a mental disorder will keep it to themselves. But if his or her diagnosis is known, then learning about the illness can aid in understanding and accepting the person. Being prepared for possible behaviors, that may or may not surface, can make it easier to support people with mental illness.

The psychotic states of my bipolar disorder can lead to religious confusion. In my highest manic state I felt as if I were somehow beyond the human realm. I felt like I had the ability to reach out to people spiritually and understand them as God can. I sometimes felt as if I were God. Maybe because God is everywhere, I amplified His presence because everything is grandiose in a manic state. Christians may be appalled by this. I was not coming from a realistic place. Yet feeling how real God is solidified my belief in God.

During another hospitalization my pastor (at the time) had to make a difficult but wise decision. He decided to discourage me from contacting multiple church members. By not giving me phone numbers and not providing my contact information to them, the contact was successfully limited. Why was this best? My hospitalizations are designed to reduce stimuli, and less contact with friends and family is necessary. I am not myself when I'm manic. I say and do things that are totally out of character. I am hospitalized to prevent me from hurting friendships by exposing people to my worst manic symptoms. So my pastor's decision kept me from straining my connections to my church family with odd behavior and communication. When I became well again, they were there for me with open arms. My pastor and his wife were there for me by phone and visiting when possible. Though phoning and visiting were limited during my treatment, the contact I had with them made me aware of Christ's closeness. This reached into the confusion and gave me peace.

"The contact I had with them made me aware of Christ's closeness."

DEPRESSION
by Siri

One of the worst parts of experiencing depression is that people seem to get frustrated when you do not get better quickly. Many who have never been in a deep depression think, "Why can't she just shake it off and get on with things?" or "Why doesn't she just get out of the house and get some fresh air?" What they don't understand is that by the time your depression is visible to the outside world, you are beyond the point where any of these simple remedies will do any good.

During my depression I went for grueling walks every day in the forest, sometimes for one or two hours, in the vain attempt to exhaust myself so I could get some sleep during the night. This did not help at all. As I got deeper and deeper into the downward spiral my prayers and songs during the walks changed. Maybe in the first few weeks I prayed for healing and help with sleep. After three months I was so ill that I started sincerely praying for death. I never wanted to kill myself, because it would have been too hard on my three children. Therefore, I prayed sincerely every day along these lines, "Lord, I can't do this anymore. I can't suffer anymore. I know You are coming to take us all to heaven in the end...So could You come now? Could You come today? I know it would have been nice to see my children grow up and get married. It would have been nice to see my grandchildren, but I just can't get through another day of suffering."

I felt so guilty, too, like I had let my friends and family down. My husband actually pointed out, "Have you noticed how when we go to church now people actually avoid talking to you? They know you're so ill, and they don't know what to say to you."

On the positive side, I did receive genuine love and prayer from several key people in the women's Bible study I attended every Thursday. I was very honest about my condition and my lack of sleep over many weeks and months. Several women made a sincere effort to give me hugs and tell me they were praying for me. This was a big boost psychologically.

My pastor came to our house on several occasions and prayed with me, which was comforting and showed my husband that the church cared for me on a practical level. The pastor even came and anointed me with oil, which was very moving. The pastor's wife gave me a beautiful pot with some pretty spring flowers. Attached was a card with some key verses that people use to combat depression. The card said, *"When you see these flowers remember that spring is coming! You will get better."* I can't tell you how much that silly pot of flowers helped me.

What are some other things a church can do to demonstrate love to a depressed person and her family? Pray for them. Provide good Christian books. Help the person find Bible verses that will bring comfort and hope. Offer to carpool their kids to day care or school. (I shudder when I think of how I endangered the lives of my children during this period. I got behind the wheel many times when I was in no condition to drive, having gone days without quality sleep.)

Another practical way to help: bring a casserole to the house for dinner. At one point the beautiful ladies in my Bible study were so worried about me that they actually got together and signed up for an entire week of home-delivered meals. I hadn't been shopping for weeks, even to buy a carton of milk, because my nerves were so shot. My husband did all the shopping, all the cooking, and all the housework, because I was like a zombie. When the ladies brought the meals it was such a practical outpouring of love that I was brought to my knees.

MINISTERING TO CHILDLESS COUPLES
by James, a pastor and husband

From personal experience, my wife and I find it very difficult (even as a pastor) to navigate church culture when we don't have children. Everything is focused on the family, and when you don't have kids it is hard to fit in, especially for my wife, because she doesn't feel like she belongs anywhere! Every conversation seems to revolve around teenager issues, children's accomplishments, how the new baby is doing, or what sports or lessons the kids are taking. Men seem to have more to talk about like sports, politics, the economy, etc. But when women congregate at social events, all they seem to talk about is how the kids are sleeping, how much they've grown, and how much trouble they are causing. That's why my wife hates to go to social events. One of the things that drives my wife crazy is women who complain about their kids or about getting pregnant unexpectedly. My wife does not come to baby dedication services; if she does, she spends most of the afternoon in tears. Well-meaning people say, "Oh, it will be her turn soon."

In a traditional suburban church, it may be difficult for childless couples to find their place because everything is geared around families: family ministries, youth camps, children's Christmas programs, father-son bowling night, kids clubs, etc. Many churches don't really even know how to classify childless couples since they are too old for the young marrieds group, they don't have kids or grandkids, and they're not single, divorced, blended, or remarried.

People often assume we have children, and start off conversations that way. Either of two things then happen. They don't know what to say and walk away when they find out we don't have kids. Or they begin to tell us how we should adopt, have in vitro fertilization, or wait it out because they had a friend who got pregnant at 43 years of age!

Here are some recommendations for churches who want to show love to couples without children:

- Redirect conversations about children to other topics so people without kids can have something to share. Provide events for couples where the focus is not on parenting or children. Take an active interest in the hobbies, careers, and ministries of those without children and plan ways to connect with them.

- Recognize that there is no such thing as a perfect or ideal family. The church is to welcome families of all sizes.

- Everyone has a home, whether or not there are children present. Make it a focus of your church to support the "home" as the foundation for ministry.

- Churches need to engage people in ministry. This means more than providing groups for divorce care and single parents, or home groups for childless couples; it means getting these folks involved and engaged in active ministry through the church. This can open their eyes to other people's issues and help take the focus off the challenges they are facing themselves. More important, it helps them connect and feel a part of the church family as they minister and serve other people in the body.

- The church should do everything it can to minister to childless couples, but the church can only do so much. Couples need to choose against defensiveness, anger, bitterness, and jealousy. Nevertheless, the church can assist couples working through the pain and disappointment of being childless and help them find a place of ministry and service, joy and fulfillment in the family of God.

HELPING SINGLE PARENTS
by Karen, a single mom

> "We were cared for, prayed for, and not left alone to fend for ourselves."

When I found myself separated, a couple from church took me under their wing for a season of time. For the first few months, the wife made me schedule time with her once a week to go out for coffee to talk about how I was coping. After a while, it was every second week, then monthly until I figured I was OK. Once a week, especially at the beginning, she would phone and check in with me to see how I was doing.

The husband would check up on me to see if I needed help financially or otherwise. I remember during the first summer when I wasn't working or getting financial support, he dropped over with boxes of food, gift certificates for a grocery store, and meat—not just hamburger, but steak! Another time, when my phone was disconnected and I couldn't be reached, he and his son drove for many miles to check up on us to see if we were all right.

For the first couple of Christmases, I was invited to their home for Christmas Day and dinner until I had a chance to create my own network of friends with whom to spend Christmas. Nowadays, I don't see this couple very often, but I know I wouldn't have been able to make it through this ordeal as well as I did without this couple. We were cared for, prayed for, and not left alone to fend for ourselves. They are still very, very special to me!

Here are some ways that churches can come alongside single parents:

- Invite the single parent to social functions, such as barbecues and parties. The church is predominately a couple's world, and people may forget about singles or presume they would feel uncomfortable in certain settings. At least ask!

- Invite the single parent and family over for dinner in your home.

- Invite the parent out for a movie, a concert, or to watch a home video.

- Invite the single parent over for special holidays. Don't assume they are with their own family, as the children may be at the other parent's place, and extended family may be distant.

- Invite the children over and help them make presents for their parents and family during Christmas.

- Have the kids over to do something special anytime to give the parent a break.

- If the child doesn't have adequate access to one parent, be the big brother/sister/mentor to that child.
- Attend special events for the children such as a graduation, concert, award ceremony, recital, or game.

- Include the single parent when enlisting people to serve in the church's ministries.

- Give hugs.

- Continue to ask how they are doing even when you think things are settled.

- Organize a work bee to help with yard and home maintenance.

- Give Christmas baking, or flowers on Valentine's Day.

What about the Homeless?

Those living on the street need to be recognized as individuals. They need someone to look them in the eye and ask their name. Some don't feel comfortable going to churches, because they don't have any money to give when the offering is taken. Others never consider going to most churches, because they have no decent clothes, or because they feel like they are a part of a subsociety that no longer belongs with "normal" people. Most cannot handle the judgmental stares, the critical comments, or the fear and suspicion they see on people's faces.

Mary was a registered nurse who worked with mentally ill people. She lived in a half-million-dollar house and drove a high-end car. She told me her ordeal began when an elderly neighbor put drugs in her tea to help her deal with anxiety. In less than a month she not only became an addict, she lost her job, her apartment, and became isolated from her family.

ON THE STREETS
by Mary, formerly homeless

If someone had a fire and lost everything, the neighbors would rally around them and provide what they need. Homeless people have lost everything, and instead of feeling compassion for us, people spit on us and throw rocks at us. I was reduced to bathing in the creek in the middle of winter. I had forgotten that I was even human; I was like a dog that went wild, because I was rejected and not fed. I had become primal. What brought me out of my drug-induced stupor was unconditional love. What brought me into it in the first place was the judgmental attitudes of others. The only people who accepted me were other addicts. They don't judge one another.

Church should be neutral turf where anyone in any condition is welcomed. What drew me to my current church was acceptance. You can roll out of a trash dumpster and walk into this church and they won't blink an eye. The reason people become homeless is often due to depression, rejection, loss, addiction, and many have been sexually abused as children. When you look at an addict or homeless person, picture them as that little boy that an uncle raped, or that little girl regularly abused by her mother's boyfriend. How would you treat that little boy or girl? Everyone has been through a version of the same thing. Remember, these people are someone's son or daughter.

When I was on the street, what I needed most was:

- *Socks.* You walk everywhere 24 hours a day. You need a good pair of socks or two!

- *Food.* If you want to befriend a wild animal, you have to earn trust through food. They will come to you as you meet their needs, and let you pet them and talk to them and tame them. Those on the street are not wild animals but they are in survival mode. They are just trying to get their most basic needs met.

- *A safe place to sleep.* I would have been so happy if I could have slept in a little room with a bed that was safe, where I didn't have to worry about being raped or robbed. On the streets, I was approached every single night for sex even though I was not a prostitute. It was never safe to sleep at night. I continued to take drugs in order to be able to function. I always had to keep moving to avoid being hurt or robbed—you can't stay still.

- *I needed someone to walk with me through the process* (government, social agencies, ministries) and help me navigate the system to get my life back on track. Recovery is the first step, then treatment.

PRACTICAL STEPS FOR CHURCHES
by Ed and Kathie Chiu, The Caring Place (a Salvation Army ministry), British Columbia, Canada

We were planting a church in an affluent community. One day a young girl walked into our church, very pregnant, with a two-year-old child in tow. She had been living with an abusive boyfriend on a small boat on a river with no sanitation or bathroom/shower on board.

She smelled to high heaven and asked us, "Do you have a place where I can take a shower? Do you have a place I can sleep tonight?" We were not prepared to help her. We live in such an affluent community, but there were needs all around us, and God laid it on our hearts to shift our focus from church planting to social ministry. We learned that as you give food, shelter, and clothes, you also build relationships and model healthy living.

You must build trust with those you want to love before they will accept more than your food and clothes.

Here are some actions for churches who want to love the homeless:

■ Educate your church members on how to love the homeless. Take your ushers to a homeless shelter; train them how to treat people who present themselves differently from the average middle-class person. Invite a worker from a local shelter to offer training on how to handle:

- Someone who smells really, really bad

- Someone who appears to be on drugs

- Someone who has small children to care for

- Someone who needs a shower and clean clothes

- Someone who really needs a safe place to stay for the night

- Someone who wants money from you to "pay rent"

■ Look a homeless person in the eye and shake their hand firmly. Maintain eye contact when you talk with them and make them feel valued and "human" again.

■ Realize that many homeless people are dysfunctional in their relationships. You will have to help them (in a kind way) know how to act in church, and what behavior is appropriate.

■ Holiness is faith working itself out in deeds. We have to see people through the eyes of God. It is not what the church isn't doing; it's what the church isn't being. Show unconditional love. Even when they are disruptive, loud, or angry, they have to feel that they can always come back and will be loved.

■ Model acceptance. Give them dignity and respect. Most homeless people will not walk into an upper-class church, because they fear judgment and rejection. Many churches have unfortunately isolated themselves, because people in need are afraid to approach them.

■ Homeless persons have suffered great loss. They have lost jobs and homes, some have had their children taken away, they have lost dignity and self-worth, and they are just looking for hope and for God when they come into a church. Don't just immediately turn them away to the Salvation Army or some other place because you think they would fit better there.

■ They often don't even know they are looking for God; they are just desperate and hoping for someone to say something kind to them. A man in our church suffers from mental illness, was hooked on drugs, and has the mental ability of a 12-year-old. On day he was sitting there just crying with his head down. I went up to him and said to him, "You're going to be OK. We love you and God loves you. Just sit and enjoy the music and remember you are special to us and to God."

■ Have a plan in place to help those who are in financial need, whether homeless or not. They often need more important things than money. Look at beginning a handyman ministry, shut-in ministry, car repair ministry, clothes washing ministry, medical clinic ministry. Maybe a nurse in your church can do a home visit to offer practical suggestions for them or get them what they need.

Serving Immigrants

Perhaps to you and me, Sam would seem a very average person in the community. But to his recently immigrated English-as-a-Second-Language (ESL) students, Sam may be the only friend their family has in the entire country. His Egyptian students call him "Uncle Sam." Others call him when they need help negotiating government regulations or find themselves caught on the wrong side of the law. Sam offers his perspective on helping newly immigrated families.

AN OPPORTUNITY
by Sam, an ESL teacher

I had the opportunity to live in a foreign country with my family for seven years. I had no choice but to negotiate the government bureaucracy, learn to shop, and try to speak the basic language in order to be understood. I have a good idea of what it is like to begin life again in a new country. It isn't easy.

> Sam may be the only friend their family has in the entire country.

Like many people, you may have experienced moving to a new school, town, or job at some point in your life. Yet no matter how different the new situation, some things probably stayed the same. But what if your move was preceded by starvation, poverty, imprisonment, persecution, war, or violence? What if finding safety meant coming to a place where you cannot understand others and they cannot understand you? What would you do with the grief you felt leaving family behind and coming to a strange place where *you* were considered strange and somehow less of a person than you thought you were?

Welcome to some of the opportunities for believers to demonstrate God's love to immigrants. The love, respect, and friendship that you offer because of Jesus Christ may identify you to some newcomers as the Christian brother or sister they have prayed for God to send. To others, your willingness to be involved in their new lives (helping with shopping, practicing the language, teaching them to drive) becomes a witness that cannot be denied. As your church deliberately shows newcomers to your country kindness, honor, and help, it becomes an invitation to discover a whole new community, the fellowship of hope in Christ.

Blessing the Chronically Ill

Migraine headaches, paralyzing back pain, arthritis, and many other physical conditions can be debilitating, frustrating, exasperating, and emotionally traumatizing. People who are normally gentle, kind, and giving can become hostile, critical, and selfish because of the pain they must deal with day in and day out. Surgery after surgery, prescription after prescription, and one experimental procedure after another can wear out a person and leave him or her longing for some faint semblance of what used to be "normal."

Different conditions require different responses. But first and foremost, people dealing with chronic pain or illnesses need serious and concerted prayer from their pastors and church leaders, and all the brothers and sisters. Many would gratefully be anointed by oil and prayed over by their spiritual elders as the brother of Jesus recommends, *"Is anyone among you sick? Let him call for the elders of the church, and let them pray over him, anointing him with oil in the name of the Lord"* (James 5:14).

As a former pastor who has ministered to those suffering chronic or long-term illnesses, let me offer two encouragements to help churches show God's love in such situations:

■ Other church members may become frustrated that healing is not coming soon enough. But think of how the individuals who are ill feel. They need reassurance that God still loves them and that He has not forgotten them. They don't need trite answers or flippant responses, such as being told God would heal them if they only prayed more; they need encouragement and support to hang in there and persevere. Remember, Paul characterizes love as "longsuffering": *"I, therefore, the prisoner of the Lord, beseech you to walk worthy of the calling with which you were called, with all lowliness and gentleness, with longsuffering, bearing with one another in love, endeavoring to keep the unity of the Spirit in the bond of peace"* (Ephesians 4:1–3). The word *bearing* means to hold oneself up, put up with, bear with, endure, and to suffer. "Hanging in there" with those you are encouraging to "hang in there" is never easy, but that is what love does.

■ Practical demonstrations of love supported by prayer make a powerful witness. A woman in one of my churches was flat on her back for weeks with severe pain. She could not clean the house, cook the dinners, fix her children's lunches, or take care of her own personal needs without severe pain. She listened to quiet music and to the Bible on cassette tapes. She was ever so grateful when members dropped by her house to deliver prepared meals for her family to eat. The church leaders also anointed her with oil and prayed over her. In God's time, she was healed completely.

Take the Time to Look Around

When I speak at conferences or at churches, many times I look out at the audience from the platform and wonder what these people are dealing with in their personal lives.

- What difficult situations are they facing?

- What devastating news did they just receive this past week?

- What stress or anxiety are they dealing with that needs to be addressed?

- What life-changing decision must they make this week that needs to be prayed over?

- What broken relationship is consuming their thoughts?

- What issues may be paralyzing them or stealing the joy and peace from their life?

I know that if I cocoon myself in my study or spend time only with healthy, happy people, I will not be the instrument God can use to show His love to hurting and searching people. Let me challenge you to go beyond asking the "How are you?" that gets the expected "Fine" reply. Take to heart Jesus' words: *"And the King will answer and say to them, 'Assuredly, I say to you, inasmuch as you did it to one of the least of these My brethren, you did it to Me'"* (Matthew 25:40). Instead of talking with the same group of people week after week, take a good, long look at the people around you this next Sunday and see who God has brought to your church.

- Who is sitting alone? Who goes home after church all by themselves?

- Are there single moms or dads?

- Do you see military personnel or their families?

- Is there an orphanage or women's shelter nearby that needs a touch of God's love?
- Do you notice anyone who struggles with mental illness or who has been chronically ill?

- Has God brought immigrants, international students, or those in need of English-as-a-Second-Language training?

- Who seems distracted, or unusually emotional or reflective?

Again, the list of people mentioned in this chapter who need the church to love them is by no means exhaustive. Many other groups could be mentioned. And we all need to be loved in the family of God.

Love is the activity of God expressed through His people. Doing something, saying something, taking someone something, offering to help, asking how you can make someone's life a little easier, taking the initiative in Jesus' name—all these are demonstrations of love. Let's get started!

■ ■ ■

From His birth to His death, everything He did was a demonstration of love.

■ ■ ■

Chapter 9

Love Restored

*This is the message that you have heard from the begin-
ning: We should love one another.*
—1 John 3:11 (ISV)

From the very beginning, Jesus had a consistent and central
message for His daily life and teachings. From His birth
to His death, everything He did was a demonstration of
love: God's love for His people, Jesus' love for His Father, and
Jesus' love for the people.

Some writers have surmised that by many of today's standards
Jesus' ministry could be viewed as a failure. He did not begin
any sustainable church, ministry, or organization. He did not
establish any foothold in any markets to sell His "product," nor
did He make any significant headway influencing the political
system or religious hierarchy during His lifetime. He ministered
predominately to the uneducated, the simple, the poor, the sick,
the crippled, and the desperate. He ended up being executed on
a cross, abandoned by all but His mother and closest friends.

When He died, He had no property, no bank account, not even the clothes on His back to pass on.

However, we know that Christ accomplished exactly the works His Father gave Him to do. *"'But I have a greater witness than John's; for the works which the Father has given Me* to finish—*the very works that I do*—*bear witness of Me, that the Father has sent Me'"* (John 5:36, emphasis mine). The Apostle John records Jesus praying to His Father later in His ministry, *"'I have glorified You upon the earth. I have finished the work which You have given Me to do'"* (John 17:4). And John records Christ's last words on the Cross as, *"'It is finished'"* (John 19:30), after which He bowed His head and died. Christ had completed exactly what the Father had intended for Him.

The First Work Is Love

According to some counts, Jesus Christ fulfilled more than 300 Old Testament prophecies regarding the coming Messiah. This is incredibly significant, but let's also look at Jesus' own words to understand what works He had accomplished on earth.

■ He had loved His disciples.
"As the Father loved Me, so I have loved you; abide in My love."
—John 15:9

■ He had kept His Father's commandments.
"If you keep My commandments, you will abide in My love, just as I have kept My Father's commandments and abide in His love."
—John 15:10

■ He introduced His followers to His Father.
"And I declared to them Your name, and will declare it, that the love with which You loved Me may be in

Experiencing God's Love in the Church

them, and I in them."
—John 17:26

- He mandated His disciples to love as He loved them. *"A new commandment I give to you, that you love one another; as I have loved you, that you also love one another. By this all will know that you are My disciples, if you have love for one another."* —John 13:34–35

- He gave His disciples an example of how to love. *"For I have given you an example, that you should do as I have done to you. Most assuredly, I say to you, a servant is not greater than his master; nor is he who is sent greater than he who sent him. If you know these things, blessed are you if you do them."* —John 13:15–17

In essence, the Father sent His Son to earth to show mankind true love. There are many gods in the world, but only one God who has revealed to His creation that He truly loves them. Jesus came to earth to affirm God's love for us. Not only did He tell us about the Father's love, He demonstrated it to His followers and then He performed the ultimate act of love; namely, giving up His own life for us. Jesus was completely successful in doing exactly what His Father intended for Him to do. He was not sent to establish organizations, change society, impact politics, or begin some marketing scheme. He came to demonstrate God's love and offer salvation to all who would respond to that love. Love has a transforming power to it—one that softens hearts and brings compassion, mercy, grace, and reconciliation. Love draws people into the presence of God.

> The Father sent His Son to earth to show mankind true love.

I spoke with an associate pastor serving in a church that had recently fired their senior pastor. He told me 20 percent of their congregation had subsequently left the church, leaving their church's finances in jeopardy. Moreover, the fallout from the board's actions was far reaching. Some members fired off angry emails and levied bitter accusations towards the church board.

> They determined to make the two greatest commandments their *only* priority.

Others behaved atrociously toward the church staff and board; others were quite happy the board finally stood up to the pastor and did what they thought should have been done years earlier. Regardless, the church was left broken and in organizational and spiritual disarray. Trust in the leadership was devastated and had to be rebuilt. Relationships needed time for healing. So, after prayerful consideration, the leaders decided it was necessary for their congregation to go back to the basics. For the next year, they determined to make the two greatest commandments their *only* priority: loving God and loving one another.

A year after the church's decision, the associate pastor's father visited him over Christmas. He observed a remarkable difference in the church's demeanor from what he had seen a year earlier. People now lingered longer in the foyer after the service, there was more laughter and deeper conversations than before, and there was a real sense of family that he had not noticed before. It was like God had placed His seal of approval on the church and His Spirit was free to bring people together once again. Jesus told His disciples, *"'If anyone loves Me, he will keep My word; and My Father will love him, and We will come to him and make Our home with him'"* (John 14:23). If only this church had thought to truly love one another in the first place, the pastor may never have lost his job.

When love is evident in a church, God lives there among His people. When there is no demonstrable evidence of love in a church, it means that Jesus has been pushed outside and replaced with something else. He stands outside His church knocking at the door, waiting for someone to let Him back in and give Him His rightful place in His body (Revelation 3:20).

> We, like Jesus, are sent into the world to live out God's love. Sometimes God's love will have the transforming effect we hope for. Other times...no amount of loving service will make our dreams come true. And sometimes people will reject God's love.
>
> Yet in sending us into the world, Jesus doesn't tell us to change people's lives. He only asks that we bear the fruit of loving as he loved. Even when results seem unlikely.
> —*Praying with the Anabaptists,* Marlene Kropf and Eddy Hall

The Book of Revelation poignantly describes Christ walking among His churches. He visits His churches looking to see how well they are representing His heart and His message. The churches that follow His commands to love one another are the ones God is pleased for newcomers to walk into so that they can experience His love for them. Churches who have abandoned their love for one another or who have exchanged it for some cheap imitation will find the presence of God strangely absent. They are not the ones that Christ is going to bless with the powerful activity of His Spirit.

"Without love the congregation ceases to be a church," writes Robert H. Mounce in *The Book of Revelation.* As harsh as it sounds, it does not matter what is printed on the sign outside the building; if a church does not know how to love one another, it cannot justify being called a Christian church. Christ came to the seven churches in Asia Minor—Ephesus, Smyrna, Sardis, Pergamos, Philadelphia, Laodicea, Thyatira—and gave them His assessment of their state of health, and then offered them an opportunity to repent as needed.

"'Remember therefore from where you have fallen; repent and do the first works, or else I will come to you quickly and remove your lampstand from its place—unless you repent.'"
—Revelation 2:5 (to the church in Ephesus)

"'Repent, or else I will come to you quickly and will fight against them with the sword of My mouth.'"
—Revelation 2:16 (to the church in Pergamos)

Most people have individually had occasion to confess their sins before God, turn from their sin, and recommit their ways to the Lord. However, it is a rare thing today to see entire churches confessing their sins, repenting, and turning back to God. But I believe in many cases this is what God is calling us to do now. And this should not be foreign to God's people. We see this type of corporate repentance, or solemn assembly, in the Bible.

Solemn Assembly

The idea of a solemn assembly comes out of the Old Testament. When God's people realized they had wandered away from His heart and neglected their relationship with Him by seeking after other gods and other interests, they corporately came together to hear God's Word and repent. This can be likened to the "revivals" that many churches schedule as a time to refocus their attention on God and to see how far they may have wandered from His standards and expectations for His church.

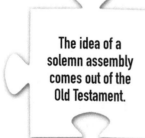

The idea of a solemn assembly comes out of the Old Testament.

On one occasion, the prophet Joel pleaded with his people to return to the Lord after they began to face the dire consequences of their sins. He asked them to gather together as one people before God and demonstrate their united heart of repentance, calling out to God for mercy.

> *Put on sackcloth and weep, you priests who serve at the altar! Go into the Temple and mourn all night! There is no corn or wine to offer your God. Give orders for a fast; call an assembly! Gather the leaders and all the people of Judah into the Temple of the LORD your God and cry out to him. The day of the LORD is near, the day when the Almighty brings destruction. What terror that day will bring!*
> —Joel 1:13–15 (GNT)

> *"But even now," says the LORD, "repent sincerely and return to me with fasting and weeping and mourning. Let your broken heart show your sorrow; tearing your clothes is not enough." Come back to the LORD your God. He is kind and full of mercy; he is patient and keeps his promise; he is always ready to forgive and not punish. Perhaps the LORD your God will change his mind and bless you with abundant crops. Then you can offer him grain and wine. Blow the trumpet on Mount Zion; give orders for a fast and call an assembly! Gather the people together; prepare them for a sacred meeting; bring the old people; gather the children and the babies too. Even newly married couples must leave their homes and come. The priests, serving the LORD between the altar and the entrance of the Temple, must weep and pray: "Have pity on your people, LORD. Do not let other nations despise us and mock us by saying, 'Where is your God?'" Then the LORD showed concern for his land; he had mercy on his people.*
> —Joel 2:12–18 (GNT)

I have watched women sing in the choir, attend prayer meetings, and participate in a church home group with their husbands while they are actively committing adultery! A man I know taught Sunday School, worked with the youth ministry, and was being sought after to serve as a deacon, all while he was cheating on his wife. I know a pastor who was having an ongoing affair with his secretary in the church building behind closed doors. These examples happen to be sexual sins, but I could list many other sins as well. For some reason, we like to think God doesn't notice or can't see or that He will overlook our "indiscretions" and still bless our ministry and service. It just isn't so. Nothing could be further from the truth.

If you were to honestly take a close look at your church, which of the two categories would it most often look like:

Loveless	Loving
• Going through the motions	• Intentional ministries/activities
• Shallow relationships	• Deep commitments to one another
• Selfish	• Giving
• Walls of protection	• Breaking down barriers
• Quick to leave after worship	• Lingering long after worship
• Silent individualism	• Vibrant socializing
• Arguing	• Negotiating
• Program-oriented	• People-oriented
• Staff-driven	• Staff-facilitating
• Members coerced	• Members integrally involved
• Threats and ultimatums	• Teamwork
• Alone	• Together
• Resentments	• Reconciliation
• Grudges	• Forgiveness
• Hurts	• Joys
• Division	• Unity
• Personal agendas	• Seeking what is best for others
• Occasional praying	• Regular prayertimes

At some point, God's people need to stop and take serious inventory of themselves to see if they have departed from God's

Experiencing God's Love in the Church

expectations. Have they been treating outsiders and even one another in a way that is displeasing, if not disgraceful, to Him? If so, they need to repent, turn around, and return to God's standards for His church. Mounce puts it plainly in *The Book of Revelation*, "Repentance is an active step. If the church does not repent, Christ will come and move its lampstand out of its place." Repentance restores the relationship with God and with His people.

James recommends to each person in the church to *"make it your habit to confess your sins to one another and to pray for one another, so that you may be healed. The prayer of a righteous person is powerful and effective"* (James 5:16 ISV). The point is this: if there is unconfessed sin, then there can be no expectation that our prayers will be effective and powerful. God is looking for people who can lift up clean hands in righteous prayer, not those whose hands are stained with sin (Psalm 28:2).

Let's be honest: there is no perfect church, just as there is no perfect family. But just as we can tell whether or not the members of imperfect families have a deep love for one another, so we can know whether or not love is present among the members of an imperfect church. The writer of Hebrews says, *"And let us consider one another to stir up love and good works"* (Hebrews 10:24). This means each person in the church should strongly encourage one another (the Greek word translated *stir up* is a word sometimes used in the context of causing a riot!) to avoid the actions and descriptions of the Loveless column (above) and move over to the Loving column.

What About You?

And above all things have fervent love for one another, for "love will cover a multitude of sins."
—1 Peter 4:8

Try to be at peace with everyone, and try to live a holy life, because no one will see the Lord without it. Guard against turning back from the grace of God. Let no one become like a bitter plant that grows up and causes many troubles with its poison.
—Hebrews 12:14–15 (GNT)

We've primarily examined the attitudes and behaviors of the church body as a whole in this book, but let's make it personal. After all, the church is made up of individual members. How well are *you* showing love to others?

■ Do you have a strong personal commitment to your brothers and sisters in Christ?

■ Have you taken advantage of some of the many opportunities to help those who have been in need in the past few months?

■ Are you holding any resentment toward people that has stopped you from loving others or do you have lingering hurts that you need to let go of?

■ Are there people with whom you need to be reconciled or whom you need to ask to forgive you?

■ Are you waiting for other people to reach out to you first or take the initiative before you will be open to loving them?

■ How many people in your church would you be willing to give your life for?

For an individual and for a church, repentance can be a good thing. It restores our relationship with God and puts our feet back on the right pathway.

Repentance is admitting that:

- We have failed.

- We have lied to God and to others.

- We have embarrassed our church family.

- We have put ourselves before others.

- We have done what is offensive to God.

- We have ignored His Spirit.

- We have walked away when God asked us to engage in ministering His love to others.

But repentance also

- restores our relationship with God,

- brings reconciliation to those from whom we have become estranged,

- frees us from sin's bondage,

- allows the Holy Spirit to use us again,

- restores the joy of our salvation,

- shows others we are just as human as they are,

- removes all the barriers preventing God's power from working through us,

- averts the judgment of God being poured out on us, and

- proves that Satan is a liar.

Satan would have us believe repentance is a bad thing, something distasteful and difficult. But the truth is this: repentance is liberating and brings freedom to the soul and the spirit. It restores joy and peace and love and grace and everything good. Repentance causes God to relent in bringing His judgment and wrath upon us. Even the consequences of exposing our sin and admitting our wrongs can be borne with grace when we have a repentant heart.

What Love Can Do

"Just as you, Father, are in me and I am in you, may they also be one in us, so that the world may believe that you sent me. I have given them the glory that you gave me, so that they may be one, just as we are one. I am in them, and you are in me. May they be completely one, so that the world may know that you sent me and that you have loved them as you loved me."
—John 17:21–23 (ISV)

As I stated earlier in the book and want to emphasize again, Jesus here prays for unity among His church *so* that the world may know God loves them too! When God's people obey the commands to love God and to love one another, the world will be able to see that God's love is real. When love is missing from the church, the world can search everywhere and find only facsimiles of love, imitations

> Simply by watching Christians around them, nonbelievers can be drawn to God's love.

Experiencing God's Love in the Church

of love, and substitutes for love; they cannot find true love apart from God and His people.

God draws the lost and hurting to churches all the time, to His body, where they should be able to experience His love in real and tangible ways. He wants love to be so obvious among His people that when a lost person comes into contact with them that lost person will immediately sense a difference. The difference is the presence of the Holy Spirit in the lives of God's people. *"Now hope does not disappoint, because the love of God has been poured out in our hearts by the Holy Spirit who was given to us"* (Romans 5:5). God has done everything necessary to help us love one another and to enable us to love others outside the church. The more we let God have His way in our life, the more we will reflect His love to others around us.

It is amazing that simply by watching Christians around them, nonbelievers can be drawn to God's love for them. My son brought home a basketball teammate from school one afternoon. This boy was in his second foster home, abandoned by a drug-addicted mother and an uninvolved father. The couple caring for him were not Christians, but seemed stable and compassionate, and sincerely looked out for his best interests. But there was something about our home life that intrigued him. Perhaps it was my wife's wonderful homemade cookies and gourmet cooking that he loved, but I don't think that is what drove him to ask if we would adopt him. He saw what a home could look like when Christ is at the center. He saw the love of God demonstrated between parents and children, something he had not known before. We let him know that he was welcome in our home anytime, and that our door was always open to him.

I spoke with a young man under the cover of darkness during a visit to an Arab country. His white, flowing robes and headdress were starkly contrasted with my dark, Western clothing. He was a former Muslim who had recently come to faith in Christ and was thirsty to know more about the Lord. His decision to become a follower of Christ meant that, should his family find out, he would be disowned and imprisoned, and his wife and children would be taken away from him.

I gave him some Christian books (which he carefully hid) and asked him how he became a Christian in an environment where it was illegal for him to convert. He said it was by watching two Christian professors at his school interact with one another. He told me that even though he was warned to avoid any discussion of religion with them, he was fascinated by the love they showed toward one another. His home environment was often hostile, angry, and threatening, whereas he saw forgiveness, compassion, and grace between these two teachers—characteristics unfamiliar to him—and he was compelled to find out more. They shared with him that Christ had come into their lives and showed them how to love others, including him. This was what was missing from his life. He smiled as he spoke, and the sincerity and intensity in his eyes verified it was true. It was by observing Christian love between two church members that a young Muslim man was drawn to Christ.

I wish every believer would choose to love like those two professors. We've got to count the cost and remember that to act unlovingly goes against everything Christ stood for.

I'd like to conclude with some select passages of Scripture that I believe should always be at the forefront of everything we do as Christians:

■ *"My little children, let us not love in word or in tongue, but in deed and in truth"* (1 John 3:18). Our actions, as they say, speak louder than our words. What we do shows others what we believe. If our beliefs do not impact our actions, we do not truly believe what we say we believe. Our actions emanate from what we believe and what we value. To our brothers and sisters in Christ, and to a watching world that desperately needs to know God, we must show love in action rather than in empty words spoken from a pulpit or taught in a Sunday School class. *"Let your light so shine before men, that they* may see your good works *and glorify your Father in heaven"* (Matthew 5:16, emphasis mine).

■ *"Let us be concerned for one another, to help one another to show love and to do good"* (Hebrews 10:24 GNT) Another translation says it this way, *"And let us consider one another in order to stir up love and good works"* (NKJV). The King James even tells us to *"provoke"* one another to love and actions. The sense here is that we should not only demonstrate love for one another, but we need to help others learn how to be excited about loving one another in practical and meaningful ways. We must educate believers about the ways of God and Christ's expectations for us. We should create opportunities in our churches for all members to strengthen the weak, encourage the downhearted, lift up those who have fallen, and hold one another accountable for any ungodly actions, words, or attitudes that would jeopardize the bond of love that ties us together. Let us no longer provoke others to wrath, but provoke them to love!

■ *"May the Lord make you increase and abound in love to one another and to all, just as we do to you"* (1 Thessalonians 3:12). Paul prayed this for the believers in Thessalonica because he knew that, without love, the church would fail. He knew love for Christ, for one another, and for all people was the foundation of the church. Wonderful programs and ministries, powerful preaching, and excellent missions programs are nothing without love. People may attend fancy Christmas productions at other churches or send their kids to other youth programs, but they will always come back to the place where they are truly loved. If your church does not yet abound in love, there is room to grow more and more.

I will add one more Scripture to the list. Read Paul's words again describing the kind of love we need to show in our business meetings, our committee meetings, our study groups, our missions projects, during our coffee time, and throughout our ministry activities.

> *Love is kind and patient, never jealous, boastful, proud, or rude. Love isn't selfish or quick tempered. It doesn't keep a record of wrongs that others do. Love rejoices in the truth, but not in evil. Love is always supportive, loyal, hopeful, and trusting. Love never fails!*
> —1 Corinthians 13:4–8 (CEV)

Let it be so in our churches today so that the world may know that God sent His Son and that He loves them with a great and unmatchable love!

Simple Steps to Revive Love in the Church: A Review

STUDY CHRIST. Read through the Gospels and notice how He treated those whom God put in His pathway. Let Him be your example.

STUDY THE FIRST CHURCHES. The first New Testament churches were great examples of what love can look like among God's people.

PRAY. Ask God what is on His heart for His people to do to show love to others.

REPENT. If you realize after reading this book that your church has been withholding love from those God has been sending you, ask Him for forgiveness and begin taking steps to change, starting with your own heart.

LOVE AS YOU WANT TO BE LOVED. Christ said we are to love others as we love ourselves. Would you like someone to drop off a meal to your home for your family when you are sick? Do that for others. The possibilities for practical ministry are endless.

RESIST BLAMING AND JUDGING PEOPLE. Blaming and judging are passive behaviors that ask nothing of you except your opinion. Ask yourself what you should be doing personally to show other people the love of God, whether they "deserve" it or not.

JUST ASK. The only way you are ever going to know how to love people you don't know is to get to know them!

SURVEY YOUR CONGREGATION. Find out the needs in your church and let God guide you to begin taking positive steps to help you love people in a practical and meaningful way.

LOOK OVER THE FENCE. See what other churches do to show love to various groups within their congregations.

EQUIP PEOPLE TO LOVE. When you start to look for people to love, you will find them everywhere! Training opens people's eyes and gives them the skills and confidence to do something practical for those in need.

SHOW HOSPITALITY. Let your own home be a place where people experience the love of God without any pretensions, expectations, or strings attached.

DO SOMETHING PRACTICAL. Doing something, anything, is *always* better than doing nothing at all! Anything you can do to show kindness and love to others is well worth doing.

New Hope® Publishers is a division of WMU®, an international organization that challenges Christian believers to understand and be radically involved in God's mission. For more information about WMU, go to www.wmu.com. More information about New Hope books may be found at www.newhopepublishers.com. New Hope books may be purchased at your local bookstore.

If you've been blessed by this book,
we would like to hear your story.
The publisher and author welcome your
comments and suggestions at:
newhopereader@wmu.org.

Also by the Blackabys

The Family God Uses
Leaving a Legacy of Influence
Tom and Kim Blackaby
ISBN-13: 978-1-59669-251-0

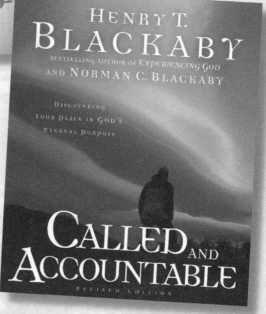

Called and Accountable
Henry T. Blackaby and
Norman C. Blackaby
ISBN-13: 978-1-56309-946-5

Available in
bookstores everywhere.

For information about these books or any New Hope product,
visit www.newhopepublishers.com.